ONE POT

ONE POT

100 SIMPLE RECIPES TO COOK TOGETHER

LAROUSSE

AMANDINE BERNARDI

INTRODUCTION
6–11

VEGETABLES
12–45

FISH AND SEAFOOD
46–69

POULTRY AND GAME
70–107

PORK
108–133

BEEF AND VEAL
134–183

LAMB
184–201

SNACKS AND SWEET TREATS
202–219

MENUS
220–223

INDEX
224–231

RECIPE NOTES
232

INTRODUCTION

There's something undeniably satisfying about the simplicity of one-pot meals—where every ingredient comes together in perfect harmony and creating a meal is as easy to prepare as it is delicious. These versatile dishes offer the ideal solution for anyone looking to save time while still enjoying hearty, flavorful food. From vibrant vegetable medleys to rich stews, this cooking style allows the ingredients to do the heavy lifting, where deepened flavors meld effortlessly.

One Pot by Amandine Bernardi is the ideal guide for creating easy and tasty meals, whether for a cozy weeknight dinner or a special family gathering. Colorful, full-flavored, plant-led dishes such as Cauliflower and Lentil Mujadara (page 16) and Vegetable Tagine (page 28) highlight the natural beauty of vegetables. Hearty meat dishes, such as the Creamy Chicken Skillet (page 78) and the Beer-Braised Beef Stew (page 148), are satisfying and full of robust flavors that evolve through slow cooking, bringing depth and richness to your table.

All recipes are clearly marked with allergen symbols (page 11) to accommodate different dietary needs. And even though these are one-pot meals, we've included serving suggestions to help you complete the meal, ensuring that you're fully satisfied with every dish. Additionally, the book features a section on Dutch ovens (casseroles) on page 8, providing informative guidance on how to use this essential kitchen tool.

Designed for both novice and experienced cooks, you'll learn how to make the most of your Dutch oven for versatile, flavorful, and efficient cooking. *One Pot* reflects the heart of this approach with meals that come together seamlessly in one vessel for serving. This cooking style captures the essence of simplicity, making the final dish easy to serve and enjoy.

Enjoy diving into the realm of one-pot cooking and discover how to turn even the simplest meal into something extraordinary.

THE ONE-POT WONDER: A DUTCH OVEN

Welcome to a world where culinary simplicity meets timeless tradition: one-pot cooking. While this book focuses on one-pot meals, the Dutch oven (casserole)—a kitchen essential beloved for its ability to create hearty, flavorful dishes with minimal effort—is at its heart. This introduction explores the history, design, and many uses of the Dutch oven, followed by tips and techniques to maximize its potential.

The Dutch oven has been a staple in kitchens for generations. Dating back to the early nineteenth century, its original black cast-iron design offered excellent heat retention and even cooking. While the material was prone to rust and breakage, modern enameled cast iron—whether matte or glossy—has remedied these issues. Today, Dutch ovens are also made from lightweight cast aluminum and durable stainless steel, catering to a variety of needs. Perfect for slow cooking, roasting, and even baking, the Dutch oven's versatility is unmatched. Its thick walls and tight-fitting lid ensure even heat distribution and moisture retention, resulting in tender, flavorful dishes. For stovetop or oven use, ceramic Dutch ovens are also an option but always consult the manufacturer's guidelines.

From rustic stews to artisan breads, the recipes in this book take full advantage of the Dutch oven's unique abilities. One of the core methods used is a two-stage cooking process: browning food first to concentrate its juices, followed by slow cooking with aromatics and liquid for deep, layered flavors. Techniques such as braising and stewing are perfect for tough cuts of meat and fibrous vegetables, transforming ingredients into tender, melt-in-your-mouth dishes. Roasting, too, begins with stovetop browning and ends with a finish in the oven, where the lid is removed for caramelization. The Dutch oven also excels at baking, such as creating bread with a bakery-quality crust by starting in a cold oven and letting the magic happen.

To elevate flavor, it's essential to incorporate aromatics and allow time to work its magic. The caramelized bits at the bottom of the pan, known as "fond," can be deglazed with liquid to create a rich, savory sauce. Choosing the right cuts of meat is also key. Beef round, neck, chuck, and short ribs are ideal for dishes like Beef Bourguignon (page 138), while lamb neck and shoulder are perfect for recipes like Lamb Navarin (page 194) or Herbed Lamb with Potatoes and Peas (page 192). Pork belly and spare ribs shine when slow cooked, and cuts of veal like shank are ideal for classics like Osso Buco (page 162). Marinating these meats will add extra depth to the final dish, ensuring a flavorful meal.

Finally, taking proper care of your Dutch oven is essential to ensure it lasts for years. After use, always allow it to cool before washing to avoid thermal shock. Hand wash with non-abrasive materials, and for stubborn stains, soak it in hot, soapy water or use baking soda and water overnight. Be sure to dry it thoroughly to prevent rust and use wooden or silicone utensils to protect the enamel. Some ceramic models may not be oven-safe or can't withstand temperatures above 400°F (200°C), so always check the manufacturer's guidelines. With the right care, your Dutch oven will continue to be an indispensable tool in your kitchen for many years to come.

DIETARY SYMBOLS

(VG) VEGAN

(V) VEGETARIAN

(GF) GLUTEN-FREE

(DF) DAIRY-FREE

(NF) NUT-FREE

(-5) 5 INGREDIENTS OR FEWER

(-30) 30 MINUTES OR LESS

VEGETABLES

PISTOU SOUP	14
CAULIFLOWER AND LENTIL MUJADARA	16
MUSHROOM RISOTTO	18
VEGETABLE SOBA NOODLES	20
SICILIAN CAPONATA	22
RATATOUILLE	24
FASOLADA	26
HEARTY CHICKPEA STEW	27
VEGETABLE TAGINE	28
CLASSIC CHEESE FONDUE	30
TORTELLINI STEW	32
EGGPLANT AND RIGATONI CASSEROLE	34
SPINACH AND RICOTTA CANNELLONI	36
INDIAN-STYLE VEGETABLE CURRY	38
CURRIED QUINOA BROCCOLI BOWL	40
COCONUT SPLIT PEA CURRY	42
LENTIL AND SWEET POTATO DAL	44

PISTOU SOUP

(NF)

PREPARATION TIME:
30 minutes

COOKING TIME:
1 hour 15 minutes

Serves: 4–6

FOR THE SOUP:

2 large ripe tomatoes

3 tablespoons olive oil

1 onion, chopped

5 cloves garlic, chopped

1 leek, white and light green parts only, halved lengthwise and sliced into half moons

14 oz (400 g) canned navy or kidney beans, drained

4 fingerling potatoes, diced

2 small zucchinis (courgettes), diced

1 carrot, diced

9 oz (250 g) green beans, cut into 1-inch (2.5-cm) segments

½ bunch parsley

2 sage or basil leaves

1 ¾ cups (6 oz/180 g) elbow macaroni (optional)

Salt and pepper, to taste

FOR THE PESTO:

5 cloves garlic, chopped

Large bunch of basil, chopped

¾ cup (2 ⅔ oz/75 g) grated Parmesan

Scant ½ cup (3 ½ fl oz/100 ml) olive oil

① Make the soup. Bring a large saucepan of water to a boil. Make a small "X" at the bottom of each tomato, then carefully add them to the boiling water. Blanch for 1 minute, until the skins begin to loosen. Transfer the tomatoes immediately to a bowl of ice water to cool. Once cooled, peel off the skins starting at the X, then seed and chop the tomatoes.

② Heat the olive oil in a Dutch oven (casserole) over medium-high heat. Add the onion and sauté for 7 minutes. Add the garlic, leek, and tomatoes. Reduce the heat to medium and cook for 10 minutes.

③ Add the navy (or kidney) beans, potatoes, zucchinis (courgettes), carrot, green beans, parsley, and sage (or basil). Pour in 10½ cups (85 fl oz/2.5 liters) of boiling water. Cover and simmer over medium-low heat for 1 hour.

④ Using a fork, coarsely mash the potatoes to thicken the soup. Add the macaroni, if using, and cook according to manufacturer's instructions until tender. Season with salt and pepper.

⑤ Make the pesto. Using a mortar and pestle, crush the garlic and basil to form a paste. Add the Parmesan and mix with a fork. Gradually add the olive oil in a thin stream, stirring constantly to emulsify.

⑥ Serve the soup hot with the pesto on the side or stirred directly into individual bowls.

CAULIFLOWER AND LENTIL MUJADARA

(VG) (V) (DF) (GF)

PREPARATION TIME:
15 minutes

COOKING TIME:
35 minutes

Serves: 4

- ½ cup (3 ½ oz/100 g) dried green lentils, rinsed
- 2 tablespoons peanut oil
- 4 onions, thinly sliced
- Generous ½ cup (4 ¼ oz/120 g) rice
- 1 small-medium cauliflower, cut into florets
- 1 teaspoon ground turmeric
- 1 teaspoon ground cinnamon
- ½ teaspoon ground cumin
- Salt, to taste
- Chopped cilantro (coriander), for garnish

① In a saucepan, combine the rinsed lentils and enough cold salted water to cover them. Cook over medium-high heat for 20 minutes until tender. Drain.
② Meanwhile, heat the oil in a Dutch oven (casserole) over medium-high heat. Add the onions and sauté for 10–15 minutes, until they are golden and caramelized.
③ Add the rice, cauliflower, turmeric, cinnamon, and cumin. Pour in enough water to cover, then stir well and bring to a boil. Reduce the heat to medium-low, cover, and cook for 15 minutes.
④ Add the drained lentils and cook for another 2 minutes to heat through. Season with salt, then sprinkle with cilantro (coriander).
⑤ Serve hot.

NOTE Mujadara is a classic Middle Eastern dish made with lentils, rice (or bulgur), and caramelized onions. This comforting and hearty dish is given a delightful twist with the addition of cauliflower, adding a unique texture and flavor.

MUSHROOM RISOTTO

PREPARATION TIME:
10 minutes

COOKING TIME:
35 minutes

Serves: 2

3 tablespoons olive oil

1 onion, thinly sliced

Salt and pepper, to taste

Scant 1 cup (7 oz/200 g) short-grain rice

Scant ½ cup (3½ fl oz/100 ml) dry white wine

4 ¼ cups (34 fl oz/1 liter) hot vegetable stock

7 oz (200 g) button mushrooms, thinly sliced

2 tablespoons pumpkin seeds, toasted

Grated Parmesan, to taste (optional)

① Heat 2 tablespoons of olive oil in a Dutch oven (casserole) over medium-high heat. Add the onion and sauté for 7 minutes, until the onion is softened. Season with salt and pepper. Add the rice and cook for 3 minutes, until translucent. Pour in the white wine and cook for 5 minutes, until evaporated.

② Add a ladle of stock, stirring constantly and allowing it to absorb. Add another ladle of stock and repeat the process. Cook for 18–20 minutes, until the rice is tender and creamy.

③ Heat the remaining tablespoon of olive oil in a skillet over medium heat. Add the mushrooms and sauté for 3–5 minutes, until softened. Stir them into the risotto.

④ Sprinkle the risotto with toasted pumpkin seeds and Parmesan, if using.

⑤ Serve hot.

VEGETABLE SOBA NOODLES

(VG) (V) (DF) (NF) (-30)

PREPARATION TIME:
10 minutes

COOKING TIME:
15 minutes

Serves: 4

1 tablespoon sesame oil

1 onion, thinly sliced

9 oz (250 g) shiitake or button mushrooms, thinly sliced

10 ½ oz (300 g) soba noodles

3 ½ oz (100 g) snow peas

2 carrots, shaved into ribbons using a vegetable peeler

Scant ½ cup (3 ½ fl oz/100 ml) soy sauce

2 tablespoons sesame seeds

¼ bunch cilantro (coriander), chopped

① Heat the sesame oil in a large saucepan or Dutch oven (casserole) over medium-high heat. Add the onion and mushrooms and sauté for 7 minutes, until the onion is softened.

② Add the soba noodles, snow peas, carrots, and soy sauce. Pour in 2 cups (16 fl oz/475 ml) of cold water, cover, and cook for 10 minutes.

③ Serve the noodles sprinkled with sesame seeds and chopped cilantro (coriander).

SICILIAN CAPONATA

(VG) (V) (DF) (GF) (NF)

PREPARATION TIME:
15 minutes

COOKING TIME:
50 minutes–1 hour

Serves: 4–6

2 tablespoons olive oil

2 onions, thinly sliced

6 tomatoes, diced

4 eggplants (aubergines), diced

2 tablespoons red wine vinegar

2 tablespoons capers

1 tablespoon sugar

Salt and pepper, to taste

¼ bunch basil, chopped, for garnish

① Heat the olive oil in a Dutch oven (casserole) over medium-high heat. Add the onions and sauté for 7 minutes, until softened.
② Add the tomatoes and eggplants (aubergines) and sauté for 10 minutes.
③ Add the vinegar, capers, and sugar. Season with salt and pepper, then cover and simmer over medium-low heat for 30–40 minutes, stirring occasionally.
④ Sprinkle with basil and serve.

NOTE The caponata can also be served in individual ramekins.

RATATOUILLE

(VG) (V) (DF) (GF) (NF)

PREPARATION TIME:
20 minutes

COOKING TIME:
1 hour

Serves: 4

5 tablespoons olive oil

2 onions, thinly sliced

2 small eggplants (aubergines), diced

2 zucchinis (courgettes), diced

1 yellow bell pepper, seeded, deveined, and diced

4 tomatoes, diced

Salt and pepper, to taste

2 sprigs thyme

① Heat 1 tablespoon of olive oil in a large skillet over medium heat. Add the onions and sauté for 7 minutes, until softened. Set aside.
② Heat another tablespoon of oil in the same pan. Add the eggplants (aubergines) and sauté for 5 minutes. Set aside.
③ Heat the remaining 3 tablespoons of oil in the same pan. Add the zucchinis (courgettes) and bell pepper and cook for 5 minutes. Add the tomatoes.
④ Return the onions and eggplants (aubergines) to the pan. Season with salt, pepper, and thyme. Cover and simmer over medium-low heat for 40 minutes, until the flavors meld.
⑤ Serve hot or chilled.

FASOLADA

(VG) (V) (DF) (GF) (NF)

PREPARATION TIME:
10 minutes, plus 12 hours soaking time

COOKING TIME:
1 hour 25 minutes

Serves: 4

---

1 ⅓ cups (9 oz/250 g) dried navy beans, soaked overnight

2 tomatoes

2 tablespoons olive oil

2 onions, thinly sliced

2 carrots, sliced into rounds

3 sprigs parsley, chopped, plus extra for garnish

1 bay leaf

1 tablespoon tomato paste (purée)

Salt and pepper, to taste

---

① Rinse the soaked beans, then add them to a large saucepan. Pour in enough water to cover them generously. Boil them for 15 minutes. Drain, then set aside.

② Bring a large saucepan of water to a boil. Make a small "X" at the bottom of each tomato, then carefully add them to the boiling water. Blanch for 1 minute, until the skins begin to loosen. Transfer the tomatoes immediately to a bowl of ice water to cool. Once cooled, peel off the skins starting at the X, then seed and chop the tomatoes.

③ Heat the olive oil in a Dutch oven (casserole) over medium-high heat. Add the onions and sauté for 7 minutes, until softened.

④ Add the beans, tomatoes, carrots, parsley, bay leaf, and tomato paste (purée). Cover with water and bring to a gentle boil. Reduce the heat to low, cover, and simmer for 1 hour. Discard the bay leaf. Season with salt and pepper.

⑤ Garnish with parsley, if desired, and serve hot.

NOTE This vibrant and hearty bean soup known as *fasolada* is regarded as Greece's national dish. It's a traditional, nutritious meal that has been enjoyed in Greek homes for generations.

HEARTY CHICKPEA STEW

PREPARATION TIME:
15 minutes, plus 12 hours soaking time

COOKING TIME:
1 hour 10 minutes

Serves: 4

- Olive oil, for frying
- 1 onion, thinly sliced
- 2 carrots, chopped
- 1 cauliflower, cut into florets
- ¾ cup (3½ oz/100 g) dried chickpeas, soaked overnight
- 1 (14-oz/400-g) butternut squash, diced
- 1 potato, diced
- 1 (14-oz/400-g) can chopped tomatoes
- 1 ⅔ cups (14 fl oz/400 ml) vegetable stock
- 1 teaspoon smoked paprika
- 1 teaspoon dried oregano
- 1 teaspoon tomato paste (purée)
- Salt and pepper, to taste
- Chopped parsley, for garnish

① Heat a little olive oil in a Dutch oven (casserole) over medium-high heat. Add the onion and sauté for 7 minutes, until softened.

② Add the carrots, cauliflower, drained chickpeas, butternut squash, potato, and canned tomatoes. Pour in the stock. If necessary, top up with water to ensure the ingredients are covered in liquid.

③ Stir in the smoked paprika, oregano, and tomato paste (purée). Season with salt and pepper. Bring to a boil, then reduce the heat to medium-low. Cover, then simmer for 1 hour.

④ Sprinkle with parsley and serve hot.

VEGETABLE TAGINE

(VG) (V) (DF) (NF)

PREPARATION TIME:
30 minutes

COOKING TIME:
50 minutes

Serves: 4–6

- 4 tablespoons olive oil
- 2 onions, thinly sliced
- 1 tablespoon ras el hanout
- 12 Yukon gold potatoes, diced
- 8 carrots, diced
- 3 large zucchinis (courgettes), diced
- 3 fennel bulbs, diced
- 2 large parsnips, diced
- Bunch of cilantro (coriander), leaves only
- 1¾ cups (10½ oz/300 g) couscous
- Salt and pepper, to taste
- Pinch of ground cinnamon

① Heat 2 tablespoons of olive oil in a Dutch oven (casserole) over medium heat. Add the onions and sauté for 5 minutes. Stir in the ras el hanout.

② Add the potatoes, carrots, zucchinis (courgettes), fennel, parsnips, and half the cilantro (coriander). Season with salt and pepper. Stir, then fill the pan halfway with water. Cover and bring to a boil. Reduce the heat to low and simmer for 45 minutes, until the vegetables are tender.

③ Meanwhile, bring a saucepan of water to a boil. Place the couscous in a bowl, drizzle with the remaining 2 tablespoons of oil, and sprinkle with cinnamon. Cover the couscous with a scant 2 cups (15 fl oz/450 ml) of boiling water, cover the bowl with a cloth, and set aside for 5 minutes. Fluff the couscous with a fork.

④ Stir the remaining cilantro into the pan. Serve hot with the couscous.

CLASSIC CHEESE FONDUE

(V) (NF) (-30)

PREPARATION TIME:
10 minutes

COOKING TIME:
10 minutes

Serves: 4

1 clove garlic	14 oz (400 g) Comté cheese, thinly sliced
2 teaspoons cornstarch (cornflour)	14 oz (400 g) Emmental cheese, thinly sliced
3–4 tablespoons kirsch	Pepper, to taste
1 ⅔ cups (14 fl oz/400 ml) dry white wine	Farmhouse bread, cut into small cubes

① Rub the garlic over the inside of a fondue pot.
② In a bowl, dissolve the cornstarch (cornflour) in the kirsch.
③ Pour the wine into the fondue pot and heat over low heat until it comes to a gentle simmer. (Do not boil.) Add the cheeses and stir with a wooden spoon, until they have melted. Stir in the kirsch mixture and season with pepper.
④ Place the fondue pot over a burner in the center of the table and maintain a gentle heat.
⑤ Serve with the bread cubes for dipping.

NOTE   This traditional cheese fondue from the Savoie region of France. Made by melting a blend of cheeses like Beaufort, Comté, and Emmental, it is typically served in a communal pot with pieces of crusty bread for dipping. This hearty dish is a hallmark of alpine cuisine and perfect for cold weather.

TORTELLINI STEW

(VG) (V) (DF) (NF)

PREPARATION TIME:
15 minutes

COOKING TIME:
35 minutes

Serves: 4

---

2 tomatoes

1 onion, thinly sliced

1 eggplant (aubergine), diced

1 zucchini (courgette), diced

1 red bell pepper, seeded, deveined, and cut into strips

6 cups (47 fl oz/1.4 liters) vegetable stock

1 tablespoon herbes de Provence or a few thyme sprigs

2 teaspoons paprika

9 oz (250 g) dried tortellini

Salt and pepper, to taste

---

① Bring a large saucepan of water to a boil. Make a small "X" at the bottom of each tomato, then carefully add them to the boiling water. Blanch for 1 minute, until the skins begin to loosen. Transfer the tomatoes immediately to a bowl of ice water to cool. Once cooled, peel off the skins starting at the X, then seed and finely chop the tomatoes.

② In a Dutch oven (casserole), combine the tomatoes, onion, eggplant (aubergine), zucchini (courgette), bell pepper, stock, herbes de Provence (or thyme), and paprika. Bring to a boil. Cover, reduce the heat to medium-low, and simmer for 15 minutes.

③ Add the tortellini and cook for another 10–15 minutes, until tender. Season with salt and pepper.

④ Serve hot.

EGGPLANT AND RIGATONI CASSEROLE

(NF) (-30)

PREPARATION TIME:
10 minutes

COOKING TIME:
20 minutes

Serves: 4

- 1 tablespoon olive oil
- 1 onion, thinly sliced
- 2 eggplants (aubergines), diced
- 3 tomatoes, diced
- 9 oz (250 g) rigatoni
- ½ cup (1 ¾ oz/50 g) grated Parmesan, plus extra for sprinkling
- Scant 3 cups (24 fl oz/700 ml) vegetable stock
- Salt and pepper, to taste
- 1 ball fresh mozzarella, diced

① Heat the olive oil in a Dutch oven (casserole) over medium-high heat. Add the onion and eggplants (aubergines) and sauté for 5 minutes, until the onion is golden.

② Add the tomatoes, rigatoni, Parmesan, and stock. Cover, then bring to a boil. Cook for 15 minutes over medium heat, stirring occasionally. Remove from heat, then let stand for 2 minutes.

③ Season with salt and pepper. Sprinkle with mozzarella and Parmesan.

④ Serve hot.

SPINACH AND RICOTTA CANNELLONI

(NF)

PREPARATION TIME:
35 minutes

COOKING TIME:
55 minutes

Serves: 8

FOR THE CANNELLONI AND FILLING:

- 2 lb 4 oz (1 kg) spinach
- 1 lb 2 oz (500 g) ricotta cheese
- 1 teaspoon grated nutmeg
- Salt and pepper, to taste
- 1 lb 2 oz (500 g) dried cannelloni tubes
- ¾ cup (2 ½ oz/70 g) grated Parmesan
- Tomato sauce or sun-dried tomatoes in oil, to serve

FOR THE BECHAMEL SAUCE:

- 4 tablespoons butter
- ¾ cup (3 ¼ oz/90 g) all-purpose (plain) flour
- 3 cups (25 fl oz/750 ml) milk

① Make the filling. Bring a large saucepan of water to a boil. Add the spinach and cook for 2–3 minutes, until wilted. Drain in a colander, then set aside until cool enough to handle. Squeeze out the excess liquid, then coarsely chop.

② In a bowl, combine the ricotta and spinach and mix well. Season with nutmeg, salt, and pepper. Transfer the mixture to a pastry bag or freezer bag for easy filling.

③ Make the bechamel sauce. Melt the butter in a saucepan over low heat. Stir in the flour and cook for 1–2 minutes. Gradually add the milk, stirring constantly, until the sauce reaches the desired consistency.

④ Preheat the oven to 350°F (180°C/Gas mark 4). Pour half the bechamel sauce into a Dutch oven (casserole) and spread out. Stand the cannelloni tubes upright, tightly packed. Pipe the spinach and ricotta filling into the tubes.

⑤ Cover the filled tubes with the remaining bechamel sauce. Sprinkle with grated Parmesan. Bake for 40–50 minutes, until golden and bubbling.

⑥ Serve hot with homemade tomato sauce or sun-dried tomatoes in oil.

INDIAN-STYLE VEGETABLE CURRY

PREPARATION TIME:
15 minutes

COOKING TIME:
35 minutes

Serves: 4

2 tablespoons sunflower oil

3 sweet potatoes, cut into 1¼-inch (3-cm) cubes

2 eggplants (aubergines), cut into 1¼-inch (3-cm) cubes

2 onions, thinly sliced

2 tablespoons curry powder or 1 tablespoon curry paste

Salt and pepper, to taste

½ bunch cilantro (coriander), chopped

① Heat the oil in a Dutch oven (casserole) over medium heat. Add the sweet potatoes, eggplants (aubergines), and onions and sauté for 5 minutes.

② Add the curry powder (or paste) and stir for 30 seconds until fragrant. Season with salt and pepper.

③ Add enough water to just cover the vegetables, cover, and simmer over medium-low heat for 30 minutes, until the vegetables are tender.

④ Garnish with cilantro (coriander) and serve hot.

Curried Quinoa Broccoli Bowl

(VG) (V) (DF) (GF) (NF)

PREPARATION TIME:
10 minutes

COOKING TIME:
30 minutes

Serves: 4

- 2 tablespoons coconut oil or vegetable oil
- 1 onion, thinly sliced
- 1 head broccoli, cut into florets
- 1 teaspoon ground turmeric
- 1 teaspoon curry powder
- Scant 1 cup (7 fl oz/200 ml) coconut milk
- Scant 1 cup (7 fl oz/200 ml) vegetable stock
- Generous 1 cup (7 oz/200 g) quinoa, rinsed and drained
- ¾ cup (5 ½ oz/150 g) drained canned chickpeas
- Salt, to taste
- Chopped parsley or cilantro (coriander), for garnish (optional)

① Heat the oil in a Dutch oven (casserole) over medium-high heat. Add the onion and sauté for 5 minutes, until softened.
② Add the broccoli, turmeric, and curry powder. Cover and cook for 5 minutes, stirring occasionally.
③ Add the coconut milk, stock, and quinoa. Stir well, cover, and cook for 15 minutes, until the quinoa is cooked and the liquid is absorbed.
④ Add the drained chickpeas and cook for another 5 minutes. Season with salt.
⑤ Sprinkle with fresh herbs, if using, and serve hot.

COCONUT SPLIT PEA CURRY

(VG) (V) (DF) (GF) (NF)

PREPARATION TIME:
10 minutes, plus 3–12 hours soaking time

COOKING TIME:
45 minutes

Serves: 4

1 cup (7 oz/200 g) dried split peas, soaked

1 tablespoon sunflower oil

2 onions, thinly sliced

2 cloves garlic, chopped

3 carrots, diced

1 tablespoon garam masala

1 teaspoon ground cumin or turmeric

2 cups (16 fl oz/475 ml) vegetable stock

2½ tablespoons tomato paste (purée)

Scant 1 cup (7 fl oz/200 ml) coconut milk

Salt, to taste

Chopped cilantro (coriander) or parsley, for garnish

① Soak the split peas in a large bowl of water for 3 hours or overnight. (This helps to shorten the cooking time.)

② Heat the oil in a Dutch oven (casserole) over medium heat. Add the onions and garlic and sauté for 5 minutes, until the onions are softened.

③ Add the carrots, garam masala, and cumin (or turmeric). Cook for another 2–3 minutes.

④ Add the drained split peas, stock, and tomato paste (purée). Stir well, then bring to a boil. Reduce the heat to low, cover, and simmer for 30 minutes.

⑤ Stir in the coconut milk and cook for another 5 minutes. Season with salt.

⑥ Sprinkle with cilantro (coriander) or parsley and serve hot.

LENTIL AND SWEET POTATO DAL

(V) (DF) (GF) (NF) (-30)

PREPARATION TIME:
10 minutes

COOKING TIME:
20 minutes

Serves: 4

1 tablespoon olive oil

1 onion, chopped

4 tomatoes, diced

2–3 sweet potatoes, diced (14 oz/400 g)

9 oz (250 g) button mushrooms, thinly sliced

²⁄₃ cup (4 ¼ oz/125 g) canned red lentils, rinsed and drained

1 tablespoon curry paste

4 eggs

Salt and pepper, to taste

Cilantro (coriander), chopped, for garnish

① Heat the oil in a Dutch oven (casserole) over medium-high heat. Add the onion, tomatoes, sweet potatoes, mushrooms, lentils, and curry paste. Stir to combine.

② Add 1 ²⁄₃ cups (14 fl oz/400 ml) of cold water, cover, and bring to a boil. Reduce the heat to medium-low and cook for 15 minutes, until the vegetables are tender and lentils are cooked.

③ Carefully crack the eggs over the vegetables. Cover and cook for another 5 minutes, until the eggs are poached. Season with salt and pepper.

④ Sprinkle with cilantro (coriander) and serve hot.

FISH AND SEAFOOD

ONE-POT SALMON	48
COD AND CHORIZO BAKE	50
EASY MONKFISH CASSEROLE	52
BOUILLABAISSE	54
MOROCCAN-STYLE FISH STEW	56
BELGIAN-STYLE FISH STEW	58
COCONUT-LIME MUSSELS	60
CALAMARI IN TOMATO SAUCE	62
THAI SHRIMP CURRY	64
SHRIMP AND RICE SKILLET	66
CATALAN-STYLE SEAFOOD STEW	68

ONE-POT SALMON

(DF) (GF) (NF)

PREPARATION TIME:
15 minutes

COOKING TIME:
45 minutes

Serves: 4

- 1 tablespoon olive oil
- 1 onion, thinly sliced
- 1 rib celery, chopped
- 2 carrots, sliced into rounds
- 1¾ cups (1 lb/450 g) canned chopped tomatoes
- Scant 1 cup (7 fl oz/200 ml) hot vegetable stock
- 2 small zucchinis (courgettes), diced
- 1 teaspoon ground turmeric
- 1 stick cinnamon
- Salt and pepper, to taste
- 1 lb 2 oz (500 g) salmon fillets, cut into large cubes
- ¾ cup (5½ oz/150 g) drained canned chickpeas
- Rice, bulgur, or quinoa, to serve

① Heat the oil in a Dutch oven (casserole) over medium-high heat. Add the onion and celery and sauté for 7 minutes, until softened.

② Add the carrots and canned tomatoes. Cover, then reduce the heat to low and cook for 10 minutes.

③ Stir in the stock, zucchinis (courgettes), turmeric, and cinnamon. Season with salt and pepper. Cover and cook for another 15 minutes. Add the salmon and chickpeas. Cover and cook for another 10 minutes.

④ Serve hot with rice, bulgur, or quinoa.

COD AND CHORIZO BAKE

(DF) (GF) (NF)

PREPARATION TIME:
15 minutes

COOKING TIME:
1 hour

Serves: 4

- 4 red bell peppers, seeded, deveined, and quartered
- Olive oil, for frying
- 2 shallots, thinly sliced
- 2 tomatoes, diced
- 1 teaspoon tomato paste (purée)
- Sprig of thyme, plus extra for garnish
- Salt and pepper, to taste
- 4 cod loins, cut into 2-inch (5-cm) cubes
- 16 slices chorizo
- 20 black olives
- Rice, to serve

① Preheat a broiler.
② Place bell peppers, skin side up, on a baking sheet. Broil for 20 minutes, until the skins are charred and blistered. Transfer the peppers to a bowl, cover, and steam for 10 minutes. Set aside to cool, then peel off the skins.
③ Heat the oil in a large skillet over medium-high heat. Add the shallots, peppers, tomatoes, tomato paste (purée), and thyme. Season with salt and pepper. Reduce the heat to low and cook for 15 minutes.
④ Preheat the oven to 400°F (200°C/Gas mark 6).
⑤ Transfer the shallot mixture to a blender and blend until smooth. Divide the mixture into oven-safe ramekins. Place the cod in each ramekin, distribute the chorizo slices and olives evenly, and bake for 20 minutes.
⑥ Sprinkle with thyme, then season with salt and pepper. Serve hot with rice.

EASY MONKFISH CASSEROLE

PREPARATION TIME:
15 minutes

COOKING TIME:
35–40 minutes

Serves: 4

2 lb 4 oz (1 kg) waxy potatoes, such as Charlotte or Yukon gold, sliced into rounds

1 lb 2 oz (500 g) monkfish fillets, cut into 1½-inch (4-cm) cubes

6 oz (170 g) country ham end, cut into strips, or smoked pork belly

Salt and pepper, to taste

Scant ½ cup (3 ½ fl oz/100 ml) white wine or cold water

① Preheat the oven to 480°F (250°C/Gas mark 9).
② In a Dutch oven (casserole), arrange a layer of potato across the bottom of the pan. Add a layer of monkfish, then scatter the ham (or pork belly) on top. Season with salt and pepper. Repeat the layering process until all the potatoes, fish, and meat have been used.
③ Pour in the wine (or cold water). Cover and cook in the oven for 30 minutes.
④ Remove the lid, then cook in the oven for another 5 minutes, until the surface is golden and the potatoes are tender. If needed, cook for another 5 minutes, until fully done.
⑤ Serve hot.

BOUILLABAISSE

(DF) (GF) (NF)

PREPARATION TIME:
20 minutes

COOKING TIME:
40 minutes

Serves: 6

- Olive oil, for frying
- 2 onions, thinly sliced
- 1 leek, white and light green parts only, thinly sliced
- 1 fennel bulb, thinly sliced
- 1 rib celery, thinly sliced
- 8 cloves garlic, chopped
- 6 tomatoes, diced
- 4 ½ tablespoons tomato paste (purée)
- 1 cup (8 fl oz/250 ml) dry white wine
- 3–4 potatoes, cut into thin rounds (1 lb 5 oz/600 g)
- Sprig of thyme
- 1 bay leaf
- 10 saffron threads
- Pepper, to taste
- 4 ¼ cups (34 fl oz/1 liter) fish stock
- 2 lb 4 oz (1 kg) firm white fish, cut into 2-inch (5-cm) pieces
- Garlic croutons and French rouille sauce, to serve

① Heat a little olive oil in a Dutch oven (casserole) over medium heat. Add the onions, leek, fennel, and celery and sauté for 7 minutes, until softened. Add the garlic, tomatoes, tomato paste (purée), and wine. Simmer over low heat for 10 minutes, until the liquid is reduced.

② Add the potatoes, thyme, bay leaf, saffron, and a pinch of pepper. Pour in the stock and bring to a boil. Reduce the heat to low and simmer for 20 minutes.

③ Add the fish, cover, and cook for another 10 minutes. Discard the bay leaf.

④ Serve hot with croutons and rouille sauce.

MOROCCAN-STYLE FISH STEW

(DF) (GF) (NF)

PREPARATION TIME:
25 minutes

COOKING TIME:
45 minutes

Serves: 6

- 3 tomatoes
- 2 tablespoons olive oil
- 1 onion, thinly sliced
- 2 ribs celery, thinly sliced
- 3 cloves garlic, chopped
- 2 carrots, diced
- 4 ¼ cups (34 fl oz/1 liter) fish stock
- 2 turnips, quartered
- 2 zucchinis (courgettes), sliced into rounds
- 2 red bell peppers, seeded, deveined, and cut into strips
- 2 ½ oz (70 g) tomato paste (purée)
- 1 tablespoon ras el hanout
- 1 lb 12 oz (800 g) cod or other white fish, cut into large chunks
- Generous 1 cup (7 oz/200 g) drained canned chickpeas
- Salt and pepper, to taste
- Chopped parsley, for garnish
- Couscous, to serve

① Bring a large saucepan of water to a boil. Make a small "X" at the bottom of each tomato, then carefully add them to the boiling water. Blanch for 1 minute, until the skins begin to loosen. Transfer the tomatoes immediately to a bowl of ice water to cool. Once cooled, peel off the skins starting at the X, then seed and finely chop the tomatoes.

② Heat the oil in a Dutch oven (casserole) over medium-high heat. Add the onion, celery, and garlic and sauté for 7 minutes, until the onion is softened. Add the tomatoes, carrots, and stock. Bring to a boil, then reduce the heat to low. Cover and cook for 10 minutes.

③ Add the turnips, zucchinis (courgettes), and bell peppers. Stir in the tomato paste (purée) and ras el hanout. Cover and cook for 15 minutes.

④ Add the fish and chickpeas. Cover and cook for another 10 minutes, until the fish is cooked through. Season with salt and pepper.

⑤ Sprinkle with parsley. Serve hot with couscous.

BELGIAN-STYLE FISH STEW

(GF) (NF)

PREPARATION TIME:
20 minutes

COOKING TIME:
25 minutes

Serves: 4

- 1½ tablespoons butter
- 2 leeks, white and light green parts only, cut into matchsticks
- 2 carrots, cut into matchsticks
- 1 turnip, cut into matchsticks
- 1 rib celery, cut into matchsticks
- Scant 1 cup (7 fl oz/200 ml) dry white wine
- 1⅔ cups (14 fl oz/400 ml) fish or vegetable stock
- 14 oz (400 g) pollock or cod fillets, cut into sections
- 16 raw shrimp, peeled and deveined
- 1 egg yolk
- Scant 1 cup (7 fl oz/200 ml) crème fraîche
- Salt and pepper, to taste
- Parsley, for garnish
- Rice, fresh pasta, or steamed potatoes, to serve

① Melt the butter in a Dutch oven (casserole) over medium-high heat. Add the leeks, carrots, turnip, and celery and sauté for 5 minutes. Add the wine and cook for 2 minutes, until the liquid is reduced.

② Pour in the stock, then arrange the fish and shrimp inside. Cover and cook over low heat for 10 minutes.

③ In a bowl, mix the egg yolk and crème fraîche. Add the mixture to the pan and stir. Season with salt and pepper. Cook, uncovered, for another 5 minutes.

④ Sprinkle with parsley, then serve with rice, fresh pasta, or steamed potatoes.

NOTE Originally prepared with freshwater fish, this traditional Flemish dish known as *waterzooi* showcases Belgium's focus on fresh, local ingredients. It is also made with chicken.

COCONUT-LIME MUSSELS

(DF) (GF) (NF) (-30)

PREPARATION TIME:
10 minutes

COOKING TIME:
10–15 minutes

Serves: 4

5 lb (2.5 kg) mussels, cleaned and debearded

2 small shallots, thinly sliced

Scant 1 cup (7 fl oz/200 ml) coconut milk

Scant ½ cup (3 ½ fl oz/100 ml) white wine

Zest of 1 lime

Salt and pepper, to taste

Crusty bread or steamed rice, to serve (optional)

① Rinse the mussels thoroughly, then drain.
② In a Dutch oven (casserole), combine the shallots, coconut milk, wine, and lime zest. Cook over low heat for 5 minutes.
③ Add the mussels, stir, and cover. Increase the heat to medium and steam for 5–10 minutes, until the mussels have opened. Discard any unopened shells.
④ Season with salt and pepper. Serve hot with crusty bread or steamed rice, if using.

CALAMARI IN TOMATO SAUCE

(DF) (GF) (NF)

PREPARATION TIME:
10 minutes

COOKING TIME:
40 minutes

Serves: 4

- 2 tablespoons olive oil
- 1 onion, chopped
- 2 cloves garlic, chopped
- 1 (14-oz/400-g) can chopped tomatoes
- Salt and pepper, to taste
- 1 lb 12 oz (800 g) squid rings, thawed if frozen
- 3½ tablespoons cognac
- ¼ bunch parsley, chopped
- Rice, crusty bread, or pasta, to serve

① Heat a tablespoon of oil in a Dutch oven (casserole) over medium-high heat. Add the onion and garlic and sauté for 5 minutes, until golden. Add the chopped tomatoes and half a can of cold water. Season with salt and pepper. Cook for 3 minutes.

② Meanwhile, heat the remaining tablespoon of oil in a skillet over medium-high heat. Add the squid rings and sauté for 2–3 minutes, until translucent. Ensure the skillet is on a stable surface and away from flammable items. Carefully add the cognac and ignite it with a long-reach lighter or match to flambé. Immediately step back. Turn on the exhaust fan and avoid leaning over the skillet during the flambé process.

③ Transfer the squid to the pan with the tomato sauce. Cover and simmer over low heat for 30 minutes, until the squid are cooked through and tender.

④ Sprinkle with parsley. Serve hot with rice, crusty bread, or pasta.

THAI SHRIMP CURRY

(DF) (NF)

PREPARATION TIME:
20 minutes

COOKING TIME:
20 minutes

Serves: 4

- 1 tablespoon sunflower oil
- 2 shallots, thinly sliced
- 1 stalk lemongrass, tough outer parts removed and thinly sliced
- 1 teaspoon Thai red curry paste
- 1 cup (8 fl oz/250 ml) coconut milk
- 14 oz (400 g) raw shrimp, peeled and deveined
- 2 zucchinis (courgettes), sliced into rounds
- Juice of 2 limes
- 2 tablespoons fish sauce
- 1 scallion (spring onion), chopped
- Thai basil or cilantro (coriander), chopped
- Lime wedges, to serve

① Heat the oil in a Dutch oven (casserole) over medium-high heat. Add the shallots, lemongrass, and curry paste and sauté for 1 minute.

② Stir in the coconut milk and bring to a boil. Add the shrimp, zucchinis (courgettes), and a scant 1 cup (7 fl oz/200 ml) of cold water. Season with lime juice and fish sauce. Bring to a boil again, then reduce the heat to low and simmer for 10–15 minutes.

③ Sprinkle with scallion (spring onion) and herbs. Serve hot with lime wedges on the side.

SHRIMP AND RICE SKILLET

PREPARATION TIME:
15 minutes

COOKING TIME:
15 minutes

Serves: 4

- 1¼ cups (9 oz/250 g) basmati rice
- 14 oz (400 g) raw shrimp, peeled with tails intact and deveined
- 9 oz (250 g) button mushrooms, thinly sliced
- 5½ oz (150 g) shallot and chive cheese spread, such as Boursin®
- 2 yellow bell peppers, seeded, deveined, and diced
- 1 small white onion, thinly sliced
- Salt and pepper, to taste
- ¼ bunch parsley, chopped

① In a deep skillet, combine the rice, shrimp, mushrooms, cheese spread, bell peppers, and onion. Season with salt and pepper.

② Pour in 2 cups (16 fl oz/475 ml) of water. Bring to a boil, then reduce the heat to medium. Cover and cook for 15 minutes, stirring occasionally, until the rice is tender and the liquid is absorbed.

③ Sprinkle with parsley and serve hot.

CATALAN-STYLE SEAFOOD STEW

(DF)

PREPARATION TIME:
20 minutes

COOKING TIME:
1 hour

Serves: 6

FOR THE PICADA:

1 tablespoon olive oil

10 blanched almonds

2 slices bread, cut into small pieces

1 clove garlic, chopped

½ bunch parsley, coarsely chopped

FOR THE STEW:

Olive oil, for frying

14 oz (400 g) live mussels, cleaned and debearded

18 littleneck clams, cleaned

6 cod steaks

All-purpose (plain) flour, for dredging

12 large raw shrimp, peeled and deveined

14 oz (400 g) squid rings

2 onions, thinly sliced

2 cloves garlic, chopped

Scant 1 cup (7 fl oz/200 ml) dry white wine

10 ½ oz (300 g) fresh or canned peeled tomatoes

1 teaspoon sweet paprika

1 bouquet garni

Salt and pepper, to taste

⅔ cup (5 fl oz/150 ml) fish stock

Rice or steamed potatoes, to serve

① Make the picada. Heat the oil in a skillet over medium heat. Add the almonds, bread, and garlic and toast, stirring frequently, until golden. Remove from heat. In a mortar and pestle (or food processor), pound the mixture until the texture is coarse. Stir in the parsley, then set aside.

② Make the stew. Heat a little oil in a Dutch oven (casserole) over medium heat. Add the mussels and clams and cook for 5–7 minutes, until opened. Discard any unopened shells. Transfer the mussels and clams to a bowl. Strain the cooking juices and reserve them.

③ Add more oil to the hot pan. Dredge the cod steaks in flour and sear them for 2–3 minutes on each side. Transfer to a plate, then set aside.

④ In the same pan over medium-high heat, add the shrimp and squid and brown for 1–2 minutes on each side. Transfer to a plate, then set aside.

⑤ Add the onions and garlic to the pan and sauté over medium heat for 5 minutes, until softened. Stir in the reserved mussel and clam juices, wine, tomatoes, paprika, and bouquet garni. Season with salt and pepper.
Cover and simmer over very low heat for 30 minutes.

⑥ Add the cod, shrimp, and squid. Pour in the fish stock and simmer for 10 minutes. Add the mussels and clams, cover, and cook for another 5 minutes. Discard the bouquet garni.

⑦ Sprinkle the picada on top. Serve with rice or steamed potatoes.

NOTE Known as *zarzuela*, this Catalan seafood stew celebrates the region's fresh fish and shellfish.

POULTRY AND GAME

SPICED CHICKEN AND LENTILS	72
CREAMY CIDER CHICKEN WITH APPLES	74
CHICKEN RAMEN	76
CREAMY CHICKEN SKILLET	78
COQ AU VIN	80
BEER-BRAISED CHICKEN	82
CURRY COCONUT CHICKEN NOODLES	84
CHICKEN TAGINE WITH DRIED APRICOTS	86
CHICKEN TAGINE WITH PRESERVED LEMONS	88
CHICKEN FRICASSEE	90
BASQUE CHICKEN	92
SOUTHWEST CHICKEN QUINOA	93
CHICKEN POT ROAST	94
FARMHOUSE CHICKEN WITH SAMPHIRE	96
TURKEY AND BUTTERNUT SQUASH STEW	98
TURKEY ROULADES WITH MUSHROOMS	100
DUCK À L'ORANGE	102
RABBIT IN MUSTARD SAUCE	104
GUINEA FOWL WITH CHESTNUTS AND PEAS	106

Spiced Chicken and Lentils

(DF) (GF) (NF)

PREPARATION TIME:
10 minutes

COOKING TIME:
30 minutes

Serves: 4

2 tablespoons olive oil

1 onion, thinly sliced

2 chicken breasts, cut into chunks (1 lb 2 oz/500 g)

Salt and pepper, to taste

Generous ¾ cup (5½ oz/150 g) canned red lentils

1 teaspoon garam masala

Scant 1 cup (7 fl oz/200 ml) coconut milk

½ bunch cilantro (coriander), chopped

① Heat the oil in a Dutch oven (casserole) over medium-high heat. Add the onion and sauté for 3 minutes. Add the chicken and brown for 2 minutes on each side. Season with salt and pepper.

② Stir in the lentils, garam masala, coconut milk, and a scant ½ cup (3½ fl oz/100 ml) of cold water. Bring to a boil, then reduce the heat to medium-low. Cover and simmer for 20 minutes, stirring occasionally, until the chicken is cooked through and lentils are tender. Season with salt and pepper.

③ Sprinkle with cilantro (coriander) and serve hot.

CREAMY CIDER CHICKEN WITH APPLES

(NF)

PREPARATION TIME:
10 minutes

COOKING TIME:
50 minutes

Serves: 4

2 tablespoons sunflower oil

4 chicken thighs

1 tablespoon all-purpose (plain) flour

2 cups (16 fl oz/475 ml) French dry cider (cidre brut) or a dry hard cider

Salt and pepper, to taste

4 Golden Delicious apples, peeled, cored, and cut into eighths

3 tablespoons crème fraîche

① Heat the oil in a large skillet over medium-high heat. Add the chicken thighs and sear for 5 minutes on each side. Sprinkle with the flour and stir well.

② Pour in the cider, then season with salt and pepper. Cover, reduce the heat to medium, and cook for 25 minutes.

③ Add the apples and cook for another 10 minutes.

④ Stir in the crème fraîche and cook for another 3 minutes.

⑤ Serve hot.

CHICKEN RAMEN

(DF) (NF)

PREPARATION TIME:
20 minutes, plus 30 minutes soaking time

COOKING TIME:
40 minutes

Serves: 4

12 dried shiitake mushrooms

4 eggs

½ cup (4 fl oz/120 ml) soy sauce

2 tablespoons sunflower oil

6 scallions (spring onions), thinly sliced

2 carrots, cut into matchsticks

2 bunches choy sum or 2 heads bok choy, thinly sliced

4¼ cups (34 fl oz/1 liter) chicken stock

7 oz (200 g) ramen noodles

2–3 chicken breasts (14 oz/400 g)

① In a small bowl, soak the shiitake mushrooms in boiling water for 30 minutes.
② Meanwhile, place the eggs in a saucepan of water and boil for 5 minutes. Plunge them into cold water to stop the cooking. Once cooled, peel the eggs and transfer them to a small bowl. Add 3 tablespoons of soy sauce to marinate until needed. This step can be done in advance.
③ Heat 1 tablespoon of oil in a saucepan over medium-high heat. Add the scallions (spring onions) and sauté for 2–3 minutes. Add the carrots and cook for another 2–3 minutes. Stir in the greens and let them wilt slightly.
④ Add the mushrooms and soaking water, remaining 5 tablespoons of soy sauce, and stock. Bring to a boil, then reduce the heat to low. Cover and simmer for 10 minutes.
⑤ Add the ramen noodles to the pan and cook according to the package instructions.
⑥ Meanwhile, heat the remaining tablespoon of oil in a skillet over medium heat. Add the chicken breasts and fry for 6–8 minutes on each side, until cooked through. Slice into strips.
⑦ Serve the noodle soup in bowls, topped with the chicken and marinated eggs.

CREAMY CHICKEN SKILLET

(NF)

PREPARATION TIME:
10 minutes

COOKING TIME:
35 minutes

Serves: 4

2 tablespoons sunflower oil	Scant 1 cup (7 fl oz/200 ml) lager
1 onion, thinly sliced	5½ oz (150 g) Maroilles cheese, diced (see Note)
4 chicken breasts, cut into chunks	1⅔ cups (14 fl oz/400 ml) light (single) cream
Salt and pepper, to taste	Rice, pearled farro, or pasta, to serve

① Heat the oil in a skillet over medium-high heat. Add the onion and sauté for 3 minutes, until golden. Add the chicken and brown for 2 minutes on each side.

② Season with salt and pepper, then pour in the lager. Bring to a boil, then reduce the heat to low. Cover and simmer for 20 minutes.

③ Add the cheese and cream. Cook for another 5 minutes, stirring occasionally, until the cheese melts into the sauce. Season with salt and pepper.

④ Serve hot with rice, pearled farro, or pasta.

NOTE Maroilles cheese is a soft, washed-rind cheese from northern France, known for its creamy texture, orange rind, and strong aroma that contrasts with its mild, tangy, and nutty flavor. For an American substitute, try Limburger or American Munster, which offer similar pungent notes and a creamy consistency.

COQ AU VIN

(NF)

PREPARATION TIME:
5 minutes, plus 30 minutes soaking time

COOKING TIME:
1 hour

Serves: 8

1 (4 lb 8-oz/2-kg) high-quality free-range chicken, cut into 8 pieces

Salt and pepper, to taste

3 tablespoons all-purpose (plain) flour

4 tablespoons butter

1¼ cups (10 fl oz/300 ml) vin jaune (see Note)

2½ cups (20 fl oz/600 ml) crème fraîche

5½ oz (150 g) dried morels, soaked for 30 minutes and rinsed (see Tip)

① Preheat the oven to 350°F (180°C/Gas mark 4).
② Season the chicken with salt and pepper, then lightly dust all over with the flour.
③ Heat the butter in a large, ovenproof skillet over medium heat. Add the chicken and sear for 5 minutes on each side. Cover and bake for 40 minutes.
④ Remove the pan from the oven, pour off the fat, and deglaze with the vin jaune. Stir in the crème fraîche, turning the chicken pieces several times to coat them, then add the morels.
⑤ Cook gently, uncovered, over medium heat for 5–7 minutes, until the sauce is thick enough to coat the back of a spoon. Season with salt and pepper.
⑥ Serve hot.

TIP You can substitute 10½ oz of fresh morels for 5½ oz of dried. Soak them for 1 hour in lukewarm water, then rinse several times before use.

NOTE Vin jaune is a unique dry white wine from France's Jura region, made from Savagnin grapes. It can be found at specialty wine retailers or through online platforms. Alternatively, a dry sherry can be used as a substitute.

BEER-BRAISED CHICKEN

(NF)

PREPARATION TIME:
25 minutes

COOKING TIME:
1 hour 45 minutes

Serves: 6

2 tablespoons sunflower oil	1 bouquet garni
4 ¼ oz (120 g) lardons	Salt and pepper, to taste
1 (4 lb 8-oz/2-kg) whole stewing chicken, cut into serving pieces with liver chopped and reserved	3 ½ tablespoons butter
2 tablespoons Dutch gin (jenever)	24 small pearl onions, peeled
1 tablespoon all-purpose (plain) flour	9 oz (250 g) button mushrooms, thinly sliced
4 ¼ cups (34 fl oz/1 liter) lager	Juice of ½ lemon
3–4 shallots, thinly sliced	⅔ cup (5 fl oz/150 ml) crème fraîche (optional)
2 cloves garlic, thinly sliced	

① Preheat the oven to 300°F (150°C/Gas mark 2).

② Brown the lardons in a Dutch oven (casserole) over low heat. Transfer to a plate and set aside.

③ Heat the oil in the same pan over medium-high heat. Add the chicken pieces and sear on each side for 3–5 minutes. Transfer the chicken to a bowl, then pour off the fat and return the meat to the pan. Ensure the pan is on a stable surface and away from flammable items. Carefully add the Dutch gin and ignite it with a long-reach lighter or match to flambé. Immediately step back. Turn on the exhaust fan and avoid leaning over the pan during the flambé process.

④ Sprinkle the flour over the chicken, then slowly pour in the beer and stir to combine. Add the shallots, garlic, bouquet garni, salt, and pepper. Cover the pan and cook in the oven for 1½ hours. Discard the bouquet garni.

⑤ Meanwhile, melt the butter in a saucepan over low heat. Add the pearl onions and cook for 20 minutes, stirring often, until softened. Add the mushrooms, lemon juice, and reserved lardons. Cover and braise for another 10 minutes.

⑥ Remove the pan from the oven. Using tongs, carefully transfer the chicken to a serving dish and keep warm.

⑦ To the same pan, add the chicken liver and the onion-mushroom mixture with its cooking liquid. Bring to a boil over high heat and cook for 5 minutes, until the sauce is reduced by half. Stir in the crème fraîche, if using.

⑧ Serve the stewing chicken with the sauce.

CURRY COCONUT CHICKEN NOODLES

PREPARATION TIME:
20 minutes

COOKING TIME:
10 minutes

Serves: 4

- 9 oz/250 g rice noodles
- 4 makrut lime leaves
- 1 onion or 3 scallions (spring onions), thinly sliced
- 2 cloves garlic, thinly sliced
- 1 carrot, shaved into ribbons
- 1 stalk lemongrass, tough outer parts removed and thinly sliced
- 1 large chicken breast, cut into chunks (9 oz/250 g)
- 3½ oz (100 g) snow peas
- 1 tablespoon Thai red curry paste
- 1 cup (8 fl oz/250 ml) coconut milk
- Salt and pepper, to taste
- ½ bunch cilantro (coriander), chopped, for garnish

① Combine all the ingredients, except the salt, pepper, and cilantro, in a Dutch oven (casserole). Add 2½ cups (20 fl oz/600 ml) of cold water. Season with salt and pepper. Cover and bring to a boil. Reduce the heat to medium-low and simmer for 15 minutes, stirring occasionally. Season with salt and pepper.

② Sprinkle with cilantro (coriander) and serve hot.

CHICKEN TAGINE WITH DRIED APRICOTS

(DF) (NF)

PREPARATION TIME:
15 minutes

COOKING TIME:
1 hour 25 minutes

Serves: 4

- 2 tablespoons sunflower oil
- 1 red onion, thinly sliced
- 3 ½ oz (100 g) gingerbread, cut into cubes
- 5 ½ oz (150 g) dried apricots
- 4 chicken legs, separated into thighs and drumsticks
- 1 tablespoon honey
- Salt and pepper, to taste
- Cilantro (coriander), for garnish
- Semolina or bulgur, to serve

① Heat a tablespoon of oil in a Dutch oven (casserole) over medium-high heat. Add the onion and sauté for 7 minutes, until softened.

② Add the gingerbread and dried apricots and simmer over medium heat for 5 minutes, stirring frequently. Transfer the mixture to a bowl.

③ Heat the remaining tablespoon of oil in the same pan over medium-high heat. Add the chicken and brown for 10 minutes, turning frequently. Drizzle with honey and cook for another 2 minutes.

④ Return the onion-gingerbread mixture to the pan. Add enough water to cover the ingredients, then season with salt and pepper. Cover and simmer over medium-low heat for 1 hour, until the chicken is cooked through and the sauce has thickened.

⑤ Sprinkle with cilantro (coriander) and serve hot with semolina or bulgur.

Chicken Tagine with Preserved Lemons

(DF) (GF) (NF)

PREPARATION TIME:
15 minutes

COOKING TIME:
50 minutes

Serves: 4

- 2 tablespoons olive oil
- 4 chicken legs
- 2 preserved lemons, quartered
- 2 onions, thinly sliced
- 2 tablespoons ras el hanout
- Scant 1 cup (7 fl oz/200 ml) vegetable stock
- Salt and pepper
- Flatbread or couscous, to serve

① Heat the oil in a Dutch oven (casserole) over medium-high heat. Brown the chicken for 10 minutes, turning frequently.

② Add the lemons, onions, and ras el hanout and stir well. Pour in stock. Season with salt and pepper. Bring to a boil, then reduce the heat to low. Cover and simmer for 40 minutes, until the chicken is tender.

③ Serve hot with flatbread or couscous.

CHICKEN FRICASSEE

(GF) (NF)

PREPARATION TIME:
15 minutes

COOKING TIME:
1 hour

Serves: 6

2 tablespoons olive oil

1 (4 lb 8-oz/2-kg) chicken, cut into 12 pieces

3 ½ tablespoons butter

24 small pearl onions, peeled

1 ¼ cups (10 fl oz/300 ml) dry white wine

Salt and pepper, to taste

12 oz (350 g) small button mushrooms

Scant 1 cup (7 fl oz/200 ml) crème fraîche

Green beans, peas, or mixed vegetables, to serve

① Heat the oil in a Dutch oven (casserole) over medium-high heat. Add the chicken and sear for 5 minutes on each side. Transfer the chicken to a bowl, then pour off the fat.

② In the same pan, melt 2 tablespoons of butter over medium-low heat. Add the pearl onions and gently cook for 5–10 minutes.

③ Add the chicken and wine. Season with salt and pepper. Cover and simmer for 20 minutes.

④ Meanwhile, melt the remaining 1 ½ tablespoons of butter in a skillet over low heat. Add the mushrooms and sauté for 5 minutes. Add the mushrooms to the pan with the chicken once it's finished simmering. Cook for another 20 minutes, until the chicken is tender and cooked through. Transfer the chicken to a serving dish.

⑤ Stir the crème fraîche into the sauce and cook for 5 minutes over medium heat, until the liquid is reduced by half. Season with salt and pepper. Return the chicken to the pan and heat until warmed through.

⑥ Serve hot with green beans, peas, or mixed vegetables.

BASQUE CHICKEN

(DF) (GF) (NF)

PREPARATION TIME:
10 minutes

COOKING TIME:
45 minutes

Serves: 4

- 2 tablespoons olive oil
- 4 skinless chicken thighs, cut in half
- 1 red bell pepper, seeded, deveined, and cut into strips
- 1 green bell pepper, seeded, deveined, and cut into strips
- 1 onion, thinly sliced
- 2 pinches Espelette powder
- 1 (14-oz/400-g) can chopped tomatoes
- 1 tablespoon herbes de Provence
- Salt and pepper, to taste
- Rice or fresh tagliatelle, to serve

① Heat the oil in a Dutch oven (casserole) over medium-high heat. Add the chicken and brown for 5 minutes on each side.
② Add the bell peppers, onion, and Espelette powder and sauté for 5 minutes.
③ Stir in the tomatoes and herbes de Provence. Season with salt and pepper. Reduce the heat to medium, cover, and simmer for 30 minutes.
④ Serve hot with rice or fresh tagliatelle.

VARIATION

For a boost of flavor, add 3½ oz (100 g) of cubed Bayonne or country ham with the fresh vegetables.

Southwest Chicken Quinoa

PREPARATION TIME:
15 minutes

COOKING TIME:
15 minutes

Serves: 4

- 2 roast chicken breasts, sliced
- 2 tomatoes, diced
- 1 onion, thinly sliced
- 1 red bell pepper, seeded, deveined, and cut into strips
- 1 green bell pepper, seeded, deveined, and cut into strips
- 1 yellow bell pepper, seeded, deveined, and cut into strips
- 1¼ cups (9 oz/250 g) quinoa, rinsed well
- 1 cup (5½ oz/150 g) canned kidney beans
- ⅔ cup (5½ oz/150 g) canned corn kernels
- 1 tablespoon Mexican spice mix
- Pinch of chili powder
- Salt and pepper, to taste
- ½ bunch cilantro (coriander), chopped, for garnish

1. Place all the ingredients except the cilantro (coriander) into a Dutch oven (casserole). Season with salt and pepper. Pour in a scant 2 cups (15 fl oz/450 ml) of cold water.
2. Cover, then bring to a boil. Reduce the heat to low and simmer for 15 minutes, until all the water is absorbed.
3. Sprinkle with cilantro and serve hot.

CHICKEN POT ROAST

(DF) (NF)

PREPARATION TIME:
30 minutes

COOKING TIME:
1 hour 30 minutes–2 hours

Serves: 8

FOR THE STUFFING:

7 oz (200 g) stale bread, crust removed and crumbled into coarse crumbs

7 oz (200 g) Bayonne ham or prosciutto, chopped

1 onion, chopped

1 clove garlic, chopped

½ bunch parsley, chopped

Reserved liver, heart, and gizzard from whole stewing chicken

Salt and pepper, to taste

2 eggs

FOR THE POT ROAST:

1 (6 lb 8-oz/3-kg) whole stewing chicken or hen, cleaned, with liver, heart, and gizzard reserved

Salt and pepper, to taste

8 carrots, chopped

4 turnips, chopped

4 leeks, white and light green parts only, sliced

Small bunch of kale, chopped

1 rib celery, chopped

1 onion, studded with 2 whole cloves

1 bouquet garni

Rice, cornichon pickles, sauce gribiche, or a white sauce (optional), to serve

① Make the stuffing. In a large bowl, combine the bread, ham (or prosciutto), onion, garlic, and parsley. Add the liver, heart, and gizzard. Season with salt and pepper. Knead in the eggs. Fill the cavity of the chicken (or hen) with the stuffing.

② To sew the chicken cavity closed, use a trussing needle and food-safe kitchen twine. Carefully stitch across the cavity opening, alternating sides to close it securely, until fully stitched. Tie off the thread with a firm knot to keep the stuffing in place while cooking.

③ Make the pot roast. Place the chicken in a large Dutch oven (casserole) and cover with cold water. Bring to a boil, skimming off the scum several times. Season with salt and pepper, then partially cover the pan. Reduce the heat to low and simmer gently for 30 minutes.

④ Add the vegetables and bouquet garni. Cook, partially covered, for 1–1½ hours, until the chicken is tender. Discard the bouquet garni. Season with salt and pepper.

⑤ Serve hot with rice, cornichon pickles, sauce gribiche, or a white sauce, if using.

TIP You can also add in rutabaga (swede) with the other vegetables.

Farmhouse Chicken with Samphire

(NF)

PREPARATION TIME:
15 minutes

COOKING TIME:
45 minutes

Serves: 6

- 3 ½ tablespoons butter
- 3 tablespoons sunflower oil
- 1 (4 lb 8-oz/2-kg) free-range chicken, cut into 8 or 10 pieces
- 2 tablespoons all-purpose (plain) flour
- 3 tablespoons sherry vinegar
- 2 cups (16 fl oz/475 ml) chicken stock
- Salt and pepper, to taste
- 10 ½ oz (300 g) samphire, rinsed and drained
- 1 cup (8 fl oz/250 ml) crème fraîche

① Heat the butter and oil in a Dutch oven (casserole) over medium heat. Dust the chicken lightly with flour. Add the chicken pieces and gently brown for 3 minutes on each side. Transfer them to a plate and set aside.

② Discard the fat from the pan. Add the vinegar, scraping up the brown bits from the bottom of the pan with a wooden spoon. Pour in the stock and bring to a boil. Return the chicken to the pan and lightly season with salt (samphire is naturally salty) and pepper. Bring to a boil, then reduce the heat to low. Cover and simmer for 35 minutes, stirring occasionally.

③ Meanwhile, bring a saucepan of water to a boil. Add the samphire and boil for 2 minutes, until cooked yet slightly crunchy.

④ Add the crème fraîche and samphire to the pan with the chicken. Bring to a boil, then serve hot.

TURKEY AND BUTTERNUT SQUASH STEW

(GF)

PREPARATION TIME:
15 minutes

COOKING TIME:
40 minutes

Serves: 4

- 1 tablespoon butter
- 1 onion, thinly sliced
- 1 lb 5 oz (600 g) turkey breast, cut into large cubes
- 2 tablespoons cornstarch (cornflour)
- 9 oz (250 g) butternut squash, diced
- 1 cup (8 fl oz/250 ml) dry white wine
- Scant 1 cup (7 fl oz/200 ml) chicken stock
- Scant 1 cup (7 fl oz/200 ml) whipping cream
- 2 egg yolks
- 7 oz (200 g) cooked and peeled chestnuts, halved
- Salt and pepper, to taste
- Rice or pearled farro, to serve

① Melt the butter in a Dutch oven (casserole) over medium-high heat. Add the onion and sauté for 5 minutes, until golden.

② Coat the turkey with cornstarch (cornflour), then add it to the pan. Add the butternut squash and cook for 5 minutes.

③ Pour in the wine and stock. Bring to a boil over high heat, then reduce the heat to low. Cover and simmer for 25 minutes.

④ In a small bowl, whisk the cream and egg yolks. Pour this mixture into the pan and stir. Add the chestnuts, then season with salt and pepper. Cook, uncovered, for another 5 minutes.

⑤ Serve hot with rice or pearled farro.

TURKEY ROULADES WITH MUSHROOMS

(NF)

PREPARATION TIME:
15 minutes

COOKING TIME:
1 hour

Serves: 4

- 2 teaspoons butter
- 4 slices turkey roulades
- 1 onion, thinly sliced
- 8 ½ oz (240 g) button mushrooms, thinly sliced
- Scant 1 cup (7 fl oz/200 ml) chicken stock
- 5 ½ oz (150 g) garlic and herb cheese spread, such as Boursin®
- 2 tablespoons crème fraîche
- Salt and pepper, to taste
- Chopped parsley, for garnish
- Chopped chives, for garnish
- Fresh pasta or rice

① Melt the butter in a large skillet over medium-high heat. Add the turkey roulades and brown for 5 minutes on each side. Transfer them to a plate and set aside.

② To the same pan, add the onion and sauté for 3 minutes. Add the mushrooms and cook for another 5 minutes. Return the roulades to the pan. Pour in the stock, cover, and simmer over medium-low heat for 30 minutes, turning the roulades halfway through. Transfer the roulades to a plate.

③ To the same pan, combine the cheese spread and crème fraîche. Season with salt and pepper. Boil over medium-high heat for 5 minutes, until the liquid is reduced.

④ Return the roulades to the pan, coat them with the sauce, and cook for 5 minutes over low heat, until warmed through.

⑤ Sprinkle with chopped parsley and chives. Season with salt and pepper. Serve over fresh pasta or rice.

DUCK À L'ORANGE

PREPARATION TIME:
10 minutes

COOKING TIME:
1 hour 10 minutes

Serves: 4

- 2 oranges
- 1 tablespoon olive oil
- 4 duck legs
- 3 carrots, sliced into rounds
- 1 bay leaf (optional)
- 3 tablespoons honey
- 2 cups (16 fl oz/475 ml) chicken stock
- Salt and pepper, to taste
- Tarragon or thyme leaves, for garnish
- Rice or semolina, to serve

① Juice one of the oranges. Cut the other orange into wedges.
② Heat the oil in a large skillet over high heat. Add the duck legs, skin side down, and sear for 4–5 minutes. Turn over and sear for 1–2 minutes. Transfer to a plate and set aside.
③ To the same pan, add the carrots, bay leaf (if using), honey, and orange juice and wedges. Pour in the stock, then season with salt and pepper. Bring to a boil, then reduce the heat to low. Cover and simmer for 1 hour, until the duck is tender and cooked through.
④ Garnish with tarragon (or thyme). Season with salt and pepper.
⑤ Serve hot with rice or semolina.

RABBIT IN MUSTARD SAUCE

PREPARATION TIME:
10 minutes

COOKING TIME:
50 minutes

Serves: 6

- 3 tablespoons sunflower oil
- 1 (3 lb 5-oz/1.5-kg) rabbit, cut into 6 pieces and liver reserved
- 6 tablespoons wholegrain mustard
- 2 tablespoons thyme leaves
- Salt and pepper, to taste
- Scant ½ cup (3 ½ fl oz/100 ml) white wine
- 6 tablespoons crème fraîche
- ¼ bunch parsley, chopped, for garnish
- Steamed carrots, sautéed mushrooms, braised cabbage, or pearled farro, to serve

① Preheat the oven to 350°F (180°C/Gas mark 4).
② Heat the oil in an ovenproof skillet over high heat. Add the rabbit and brown for 3–4 minutes on each side.
③ Generously coat the rabbit pieces with mustard. Sprinkle with thyme and lightly season with salt and pepper. Cover and cook in the oven for 30 minutes.
④ Remove the pan from the oven. Transfer the rabbit pieces to a plate, scraping off all the mustard and adding it back to the pan.
⑤ Add the wine and simmer over medium heat for 1–2 minutes. Stir in the crème fraîche and bring to a boil, scraping up the brown bits from the bottom of the pan with a wooden spoon. Season with salt and pepper.
⑥ Add the rabbit and liver. Cover, then cook in the oven for another 10 minutes, until cooked through. If it seems too runny, remove the lid from the pan before the end of cooking to thicken it slightly.
⑦ Arrange the rabbit on a serving dish. Slice the liver and add it to the dish. Ladle the sauce on top and sprinkle with chopped parsley.
⑧ Serve hot with steamed carrots, sautéed mushrooms, braised cabbage, or pearled farro.

GUINEA FOWL WITH CHESTNUTS AND PEAS

(GF)

PREPARATION TIME:
10 minutes

COOKING TIME:
1 hour 25 minutes

Serves: 4

1¾ oz (50 g) garlic and herb cheese spread, such as Boursin®

Salt, to taste

1 (3-lb/1.3-kg) guinea fowl or 2 Cornish game hens

2 tablespoons olive oil

5 shallots, chopped

3 cloves garlic, unpeeled

7 oz (200 g) smoked lardons

Pepper, to taste

14¾ oz (420 g) large cooked and peeled chestnuts

Scant 1 cup (9 oz/250 g) fresh or frozen peas

① Mix the cheese spread with a pinch of salt. Brush the inside of the guinea fowl cavity (or Cornish game hens) with the mixture.

② Heat the oil in a Dutch oven (casserole) over medium-high heat. Add the guinea fowl and brown on all sides for 4 minutes total. Add the shallots, garlic, and lardons. Pour in ½ cup (4 fl oz/120 ml) of cold water. Season with salt and pepper. Bring to a boil, then reduce the heat to low. Cover and simmer for 45 minutes, until cooked through.

③ Add the chestnuts and cook for another 15 minutes. Add the peas and cook for another 20 minutes. Season with salt and pepper.

④ Serve hot.

PORK

LENTIL AND SAUSAGE SOUP	110
SAUSAGES AND SAUERKRAUT	112
MEXICAN-STYLE SOUP	114
PULLED PORK	116
QUICK AND EASY CASSOULET	118
STUFFED ZUCCHINI AND TOMATOES	120
PORCHETTA WITH MINTED PEAS	122
PORK TENDERLOIN IN CREAM SAUCE	124
LENTIL STEW WITH SALT PORK AND SAUSAGES	126
GARLIC-SAGE PORK ROAST	128
PORK TENDERLOIN WITH ORANGE-HONEY GLAZE	130
COLOMBO-SPICED PORK AND SWEET POTATO STEW	132

LENTIL AND SAUSAGE SOUP

PREPARATION TIME:
20 minutes

COOKING TIME:
55 minutes

Serves: 4

1 large smoked sausage, such as andouille or kielbasa

2 tablespoons sunflower oil

2 ribs celery, diced

1 carrot, diced

1 onion, diced

Generous 1 cup (9 oz/250 g) dried French (Puy) lentils, rinsed

2 bay leaves

6¼ cups (50 fl oz/1.5 liters) vegetable stock

¼ bunch parsley, chopped

① Bring water to a boil in a Dutch oven (casserole). Add the sausage, cover, and reduce the heat to low. Cook for 15 minutes, until cooked through. When cool enough to handle, slice the sausage.

② Heat the oil in the same pan over low heat. Add the celery, carrot, and onion and sauté for 5 minutes. Add the sausages and cook for another 5 minutes.

③ Add the lentils, bay leaves, and stock. Cover, then bring to a boil. Reduce the heat to medium-low and simmer for 30 minutes, until the lentils are tender. Discard the bay leaves.

④ Put 2 ladles of the soup in a blender and blend until smooth. Return the mixture to the pan for a creamy consistency.

⑤ Sprinkle with parsley and serve.

SAUSAGES AND SAUERKRAUT

(DF) (GF) (NF)

PREPARATION TIME:
10 minutes

COOKING TIME:
2 hours 15 minutes

Serves: 6

- 3 tablespoons lard
- 2 onions, thinly sliced
- 2 lb 12 oz (1.2 kg) sauerkraut, rinsed and thoroughly drained
- 10 juniper berries
- 1 lb 2 oz (500 g) salted and smoked pork shoulder
- 10 ½ oz (300 g) slab smoked bacon, cut into 1½–2 inch (4–5 cm) pieces
- 2 Montbéliard or smoked kielbasa sausages
- 3 cups (25 fl oz/750 ml) Riesling wine
- 1¼ cups (10 fl oz/300 ml) vegetable stock
- 14 oz (400 g) small waxy potatoes
- 6 Strasbourg or andouille sausages

① Heat the lard in a Dutch oven (casserole) over medium-high heat. Add the onions and sauté for 7 minutes, until softened. Add the sauerkraut, juniper berries, pork shoulder, bacon, and Montbéliard (or kielbasa) sausages. Pour in the wine and stock. Bring to a boil, then reduce the heat to low. Cover and simmer for 1½ hours.

② Add the potatoes, cover, and cook for 20 minutes, until tender. Add the Strasbourg (or andouille) sausages, cover, and cook for another 15 minutes, until cooked through.

③ Serve hot.

MEXICAN-STYLE SOUP

(DF) (GF) (NF)

PREPARATION TIME:
15 minutes

COOKING TIME:
45 minutes

Serves: 4

- 1 tablespoon olive oil
- 3 ½ oz (100 g) Mexican chorizo, cut into cubes
- 1 carrot, coarsely chopped
- 1 red onion, coarsely chopped
- 1 leek, white and light green parts only, sliced
- 1 rib celery, coarsely chopped
- 1 red bell pepper, seeded, deveined, and chopped
- 1 teaspoon ground cumin
- 1 teaspoon paprika
- ¼ teaspoon red pepper flakes
- ¾ cup (7 oz/200 g) canned chopped tomatoes
- 1 teaspoon dried oregano
- 1 (14-oz/400-g) can kidney beans, drained
- Salt and pepper, to taste
- 1 (5 ½-oz/150-g) can corn kernels, drained
- Cilantro (coriander), chopped
- Corn tortillas, to serve

① Heat the oil in a Dutch oven (casserole) over medium heat. Add the chorizo, carrot, onion, leek, celery, and bell pepper and sauté for 10 minutes. Add the cumin, paprika, and red pepper flakes and cook for another 2 minutes.

② Stir in the tomatoes, oregano, and 6 cups (47 fl oz/1.4 liters) of cold water. Bring to a boil, then reduce the heat to medium-low. Cover and gently simmer for 20 minutes. Add the kidney beans and cook for another 10 minutes, until the flavors meld.

③ Put 3 ladles of beans in a blender and blend until smooth. Return the mixture to the pan. Season with salt and pepper.

④ Add the corn, then sprinkle with cilantro (coriander), and serve with corn tortillas.

VARIATION
You can substitute chickpeas for the kidney beans.

PULLED PORK

(DF) (NF)

PREPARATION TIME:
10 minutes

COOKING TIME:
5–6 hours

Serves: 4

2 tablespoons sunflower oil

1 lb 12 oz (800 g) pork shoulder or Boston butt

2 red onions, thinly sliced

½ cup (4 fl oz/120 ml) barbecue sauce

4 tablespoons ketchup

2 tablespoons honey

① Preheat the oven to 250°F (120°C/Gas mark ½).
② Heat the oil in a Dutch oven (casserole) over medium-high heat. Add the pork and brown on all sides for 7–10 minutes total. Add the onions.
③ In a bowl, combine the barbecue sauce, ketchup, and honey and mix well. Pour the mixture over the pork and onions, coating the meat thoroughly.
④ Cover and roast in the oven for 3 hours. Flip the meat and roast for another 2–3 hours, until the pork can be easily shredded with a fork.
⑤ Serve hot.

TIP Pulled pork can be used in a variety of ways, such as a filling for sandwiches, a topping for shepherd's pie, or spread on toast for a tasty snack.

QUICK AND EASY CASSOULET

(DF) (GF) (NF)

PREPARATION TIME:
10 minutes

COOKING TIME:
30 minutes

Serves: 4

- 1 onion, chopped
- 3 ½ oz (100 g) lardons
- 1 (14-oz/400-g) can white beans, drained
- 4 Toulouse sausages
- 2 confit duck legs
- 1 carrot, sliced into rounds
- 2 cloves garlic, unpeeled
- 2 whole cloves
- 1 bay leaf
- 1 bouquet garni
- 1¼ cups (10 fl oz/300 ml) vegetable stock
- Salt and pepper, to taste

① In a Dutch oven (casserole), combine the onion and lardons and sauté over medium heat for 5 minutes.

② Add the drained beans, sausages, duck, carrot, garlic, cloves, bay leaf, bouquet garni, and stock. Season with salt and pepper. Bring to a boil, then reduce the heat to medium-low. Cover and simmer for 25 minutes, until the sausages are cooked through. Discard the bay leaf and bouquet garni.

③ Serve hot.

Stuffed Zucchini and Tomatoes

(DF) (GF) (NF)

PREPARATION TIME:
15 minutes

COOKING TIME:
40 minutes

Serves: 4

4 large tomatoes

4 globe zucchinis (courgettes)

1¼ cups (8½ oz/240 g) rice

1 lb 5 oz (600 g) ground pork or combination of pork and veal

1 onion, chopped

½ bunch parsley, chopped

Salt and pepper, to taste

1⅔ cups (14 fl oz/400 ml) vegetable stock

① Cut off the tops of the tomatoes and zucchinis (courgettes). Using a sharp paring knife and spoon, hollow out the vegetables. Set aside the tops. Chop the zucchini flesh. In a bowl, combine the zucchini flesh, tomato pulp, and rice. Set aside.

② In a large bowl, combine the ground meat, onion, and parsley. Season with salt and pepper. Fill the hollowed vegetables evenly with this mixture and replace the caps.

③ Spread out the rice mixture in a Dutch oven (casserole). Pour in the stock. Arrange the stuffed vegetables on top. Cover and simmer over low heat for 35–40 minutes. If the dish appears dry, add a little water during cooking.

④ Serve hot.

PORCHETTA WITH MINTED PEAS

(GF) (NF)

PREPARATION TIME:
25 minutes

COOKING TIME:
2 hours 15 minutes

Serves: 6–8

- 1 (4-lb/1.8-kg) boneless Boston butt, butterflied
- Fleur de sel and pepper, to taste
- 3 cloves garlic, crushed
- 3 sprigs rosemary, chopped
- 1 sheet pork rind
- Olive oil, for frying
- 2 tablespoons salted butter
- 3 onions, thinly sliced
- 3 lb 5 oz (1.5 kg) fresh peas, shelled
- 1 tablespoon sugar
- 3 sprigs mint, leaves only

① Preheat the oven to 300°F (150°C/Gas mark 2).

② Season the inside of the butterflied pork with fleur de sel and pepper. Scatter the garlic and rosemary on top and roll the meat up tightly. Wrap in the pork rind, and tie with kitchen twine.

③ Heat a little oil in a Dutch oven (casserole) over medium-high heat. Add the rolled pork and brown on all sides for 5 minutes total. Add a scant ½ cup (3½ fl oz/100 ml) of water, cover, and cook in the oven for 2 hours.

④ Meanwhile, melt the butter in a saucepan over medium heat. Add the onions and sauté for 5 minutes without coloring. Stir in the peas, sugar, and mint leaves. Cover with water. Season with fleur de sel and pepper. Cover and bring to a boil over high heat. Reduce the heat to medium-low and simmer for 10 minutes. Uncover and cook for another 10 minutes.

⑤ Raise the oven temperature to 400°F (200°C/Gas mark 6). Uncover and cook the porchetta for another 10 minutes. Set aside to rest for 3 minutes, then slice.

⑥ Serve with the minted peas.

PORK TENDERLOIN IN CREAM SAUCE

(GF) (NF)

PREPARATION TIME:
20 minutes

COOKING TIME:
35 minutes

Serves: 4

2 tablespoons olive oil

1 lb 12 oz (800 g) pork tenderloin

Scant ½ cup (3 ½ fl oz/100 ml) dry white wine

2 shallots, thinly sliced

14 oz (400 g) button mushrooms, thinly sliced

1 tablespoon mustard

1 cup (8 fl oz/250 ml) whipping cream

Salt and pepper, to taste

Chopped parsley, for garnish

Fresh pasta, to serve

① Heat the oil in a Dutch oven (casserole) over medium-high heat. Add the pork and brown on all sides for 5 minutes total. Transfer the meat to a plate and set aside.

② Pour half the wine into the pan, scraping up the brown bits from the bottom of the pan. Add the shallots and cook for 3 minutes, until the liquid is reduced. Stir in the mushrooms and cook for 5 minutes.

③ Transfer the tenderloin to a cutting board. Slice into medallions, about ¾ inch (2 cm) thick.

④ Combine the mustard and cream, then add the mixture to the pan. Pour in the remaining wine and medallions. Cover and bring to a boil. Reduce the heat to low and simmer for 10 minutes. Turn the medallions over and cook for another 10 minutes. Season with salt and pepper.

⑤ Sprinkle with parsley and serve with fresh pasta.

LENTIL STEW WITH SALT PORK AND SAUSAGES

(DF) (GF) (NF)

PREPARATION TIME:
10 minutes

COOKING TIME:
2 hours 15 minutes

Serves: 6–8

- 1 lb 12 oz (800 g) salt pork
- 6 smoked sausages, such as kielbasa, pricked
- 2 rashers bacon
- 3 carrots, sliced into rounds
- 2 onions, each studded with 1 whole clove
- 1 bouquet garni
- Salt and pepper, to taste
- 2¼ cups (1 lb 2 oz/500 g) dried green lentils, rinsed
- Mustard, to serve

① In a Dutch oven (casserole), combine the salt pork, sausages, and bacon. Cover with water, then bring to a boil. Reduce the heat to medium-low and simmer for 15 minutes. Transfer the meat to a plate and set aside. Discard the water and rinse the pan.

② Return the meat to the pan, then add the carrots, onions, and bouquet garni. Season with salt and pepper. Add enough water to cover. Bring to a boil, then reduce the heat to medium-low. Cover and simmer for 1½ hours.

③ Add the lentils and cook for another 30 minutes, adding a little water if the mixture appears dry. Remove the onions and bouquet garni and discard. If desired, slice the meat.

④ Serve with mustard.

GARLIC-SAGE PORK ROAST

(GF) (NF) (-5)

PREPARATION TIME:
10 minutes

COOKING TIME:
1 hour 30 minutes

Serves: 4–6

1 (3-lb/1.3-kg) pork roast, tied

2 sprigs sage, leaves only

3 cups (25 fl oz/750 ml) milk

Salt, to taste

5 cloves garlic

Fresh pasta, to serve

① Preheat the oven to 400°F (200°C/Gas mark 6).
② Place the roast in a pan. Insert a few sage leaves between the twine and the pork roast. Scatter more leaves on top. Pour in the milk and generously season with salt.
③ Scatter the remaining sage leaves and the garlic around the pork. Cover and cook in the oven for 1½ hours.
④ Serve hot with fresh pasta.

Pork Tenderloin with Orange-Honey Glaze

(DF) (GF) (NF)

PREPARATION TIME:
10 minutes

COOKING TIME:
40 minutes

Serves: 4

- 3 oranges
- 2 tablespoons sunflower oil
- 1 onion, thinly sliced
- 1 lb 12 oz (800 g) pork tenderloin
- 3 tablespoons honey
- Scant ½ cup (3 ½ fl oz/100 ml) dry white wine
- 1 teaspoon ground star anise
- 1 teaspoon ground cinnamon
- Salt and pepper, to taste
- Parsley, for garnish (optional)
- Carrot purée, to serve

① Zest an orange. Juice all 3. Set aside.

② Heat the oil in a Dutch oven (casserole) over medium-high heat. Add the onion and sauté for 5 minutes, until golden. Add the pork tenderloin and brown on all sides for 5 minutes total.

③ Add the orange zest and juice, honey, wine, star anise, and cinnamon. Season with salt and pepper. Bring to a boil, then reduce the heat to low. Cover and simmer for 30 minutes, checking occasionally.

④ Transfer the tenderloin to a cutting board. Slice into thick medallions and plate.

⑤ Ladle the sauce over the medallions. Garnish with parsley, if using, and serve with carrot purée.

COLOMBO-SPICED PORK AND SWEET POTATO STEW

PREPARATION TIME:
15 minutes

COOKING TIME:
1 hour 20 minutes

Serves: 4

- 1 tablespoon olive oil
- 1 lb 12 oz (800 g) braising pork, cut into cubes
- 1 onion, thinly sliced
- 2 cloves garlic, chopped
- 1 (14-oz/400-g) can chopped tomatoes
- 1 eggplant (aubergine), diced
- 1 zucchini (courgette), diced
- 2 teaspoons Colombo powder (see Note)
- 2 cups (16 fl oz/475 ml) vegetable stock
- Salt and pepper, to taste
- 1 lb 2 oz (500 g) sweet potatoes, diced
- Juice of 1 lime
- Rice, to serve

① Heat the oil in a Dutch oven (casserole) over high heat. Add the pork and brown for 5 minutes. Add the onion and garlic and sauté for 3 minutes.

② Add the tomatoes, eggplant (aubergine), zucchini (courgette), Colombo powder, and stock. Season with salt and pepper. Top up with enough water to cover the contents of the pan, cover, and bring to a boil. Reduce the heat to low and simmer for 40 minutes.

③ Add the sweet potatoes and cook, uncovered, for 30 minutes, until the pork and sweet potatoes are tender. Stir in the lime juice. Season with salt and pepper.

④ Serve with rice.

NOTE Pork Colombo is a flavorful French West Indies stew made with tender pork and a blend of aromatic spices and vegetables. If you cannot find Colombo spice powder, you can use curry powder or garam masala.

BEEF AND VEAL

BEEF NOODLE SOUP	136
BEEF BOURGUIGNON	138
POT-AU-FEU	140
WEST AFRICAN-STYLE BEEF STEW	141
FLEMISH BEEF STEW	142
BEEF WITH CARROTS	144
QUICK AND EASY CHILI CON CARNE	146
BEER-BRAISED BEEF STEW	148
CREAMY BEEF WITH POTATOES	150
HUNGARIAN GOULASH	152
LASAGNA CASSEROLE	154
BEEF HOT POT	156
PROVENÇAL BEEF STEW	158
BEEF BIRYANI	160
OSSO BUCO	162
VEAL BLANQUETTE	164
VEAL AND CHORIZO BEAN STEW	166
VEAL AND MUSHROOM TAGLIATELLE	168
CREAMY VEAL AND VEGETABLE STEW	170
BRAISED VEAL WITH CARROTS AND WALNUTS	172
BEER-BRAISED VEAL ROULADES	174
VEAL MARENGO	176
BASQUE-STYLE VEAL STEW	178
FLEMISH VEAL STEW	180
COCONUT-MANGO VEAL CURRY	182

BEEF NOODLE SOUP

PREPARATION TIME:
15 minutes

COOKING TIME:
15 minutes

Serves: 4

- 2 tablespoons sunflower oil
- 1 onion, thinly sliced
- 1 tablespoon grated ginger
- 4 carrots, cut into thin strips
- 1 teaspoon chili powder
- 2 heads bok choy, halved lengthwise
- 6 cups (47 fl oz/1.4 liters) beef stock
- 6 tablespoons soy sauce
- 7 oz (200 g) wheat noodles
- 1 lb 2 oz (500 g) round steak, thinly sliced
- Chopped cilantro (coriander), for garnish

① Heat the oil in a Dutch oven (casserole) over medium-high heat. Add the onion and ginger and sauté for 7 minutes, until the onion is softened. Add the carrots and chili powder. Increase the heat to high and sauté for 2 minutes.

② Add the bok choy, stock, and soy sauce. Bring to a boil. Add the noodles and cook according to the package instructions.

③ Add the meat and gently simmer over medium-low heat for another 2 minutes.

④ Garnish with chopped cilantro (coriander), then serve.

BEEF BOURGUIGNON

DF NF

PREPARATION TIME:
20 minutes

COOKING TIME:
2 hours 45 minutes

Serves: 4–6

2 tablespoons sunflower oil

2 lb 12 oz (1.2 kg) chuck roast (braising steak), cut into 2-inch (5-cm) chunks

6–8 rashers bacon, thinly sliced

2 carrots, sliced into rounds

2 large onions, sliced

Salt and pepper, to taste

2 tablespoons all-purpose (plain) flour

2 ½ cups (20 fl oz/600 ml) Burgundy red wine

1 clove garlic, crushed

1 bouquet garni

2 ⅔ cups (7 oz/200 g) thinly sliced button mushrooms

Steamed potatoes, long pasta, rice, or green beans, to serve

① Heat the oil in a Dutch oven (casserole) over medium-high heat. Add the beef and brown for 2–3 minutes on each side. Add the bacon, carrots, and onions. Reduce the heat to low and sauté for 2–3 minutes. Season with salt and pepper.

② Sprinkle in the flour, stir, and toast for 1–2 minutes. Pour in the wine and a scant 1 cup (7 fl oz/200 ml) of cold water. Add the garlic, bouquet garni, and mushrooms. Stir, cover, and simmer for 2½ hours, until the beef is tender.

③ Discard the bouquet garni and season with salt and pepper.

④ Serve with potatoes, pasta, rice, or green beans.

POT-AU-FEU

(DF) (GF) (NF)

PREPARATION TIME:
30 minutes

COOKING TIME:
4 hours

Serves: 6

- 1 lb 2 oz (500 g) beef plate
- 1 lb 2 oz (500 g) beef shank
- 1 lb 2 oz (500 g) beef chuck roll (scoter steak)
- 1 onion, studded with whole cloves
- 4 cloves garlic, crushed
- 1 bouquet garni
- 6–8 black peppercorns
- 1 tablespoon coarse sea salt, plus extra for sprinkling
- 5 carrots, cut into large chunks
- 5 turnips, cut into large chunks
- 4 leeks, white part only, cut into large chunks
- 3 parsnips, cut into large chunks
- 2 ribs celery, cut into large chunks
- 4 marrow bones
- Cornichon pickles, to serve
- Mustard, to serve
- Toast, to serve

① Place the meat in a stockpot. Pour in 10½ cups (85 fl oz/2.5 liters) of cold water and bring to a boil. (This should take at least 10 minutes.) Reduce the heat to low and simmer for 1 hour, occasionally skimming the scum off the surface.

② Add the onion, garlic, bouquet garni, peppercorns, and salt. Bring back to a boil, then reduce the heat to medium-low. Cover and simmer for another 2 hours, skimming from time to time.

③ Add the carrots, turnips, leeks, parsnips, and celery and cook for another 30 minutes.

④ Add the marrow bones and cook for another 30 minutes. Occasionally, lay a paper towel on the surface of the broth to absorb any fat and discard.

⑤ Using a slotted spoon, transfer the meat, marrow bones, and vegetables to a large serving dish. Strain the broth into a soup tureen. Drizzle the contents of the dish with 2–3 tablespoons of broth. Season with salt.

⑥ Serve with cornichon pickles, mustard, and toast for the marrow bones.

West African-Style Beef Stew

(DF) (GF)

PREPARATION TIME:
15 minutes

COOKING TIME:
1 hour

Serves: 4

- 2 tablespoons sunflower oil
- 1 onion, thinly sliced
- 2 cloves garlic, chopped
- 1 tablespoon grated ginger
- 1 lb 5 oz (600 g) chuck steak, cut into bite-sized cubes
- 4 sweet potatoes, diced
- 4 tablespoons tomato paste (purée)
- 1 teaspoon mild chili powder
- 2 cups (16 fl oz/475 ml) chicken stock
- Salt and pepper, to taste
- 5 tablespoons peanut butter
- Rice, to serve

① Heat the oil in a Dutch oven (casserole) over medium heat. Add the onion, garlic, and ginger and sauté for 7 minutes, until the onion is softened. Add the beef and brown for 3 minutes on each side.

② Add the sweet potatoes, tomato paste (purée), and chili powder. Pour in the stock, then season with salt and pepper. Mix well, cover, and bring to a boil. Reduce the heat to low and simmer for 40 minutes.

③ Stir in the peanut butter and cook for another 2–3 minutes.

④ Serve hot with rice.

NOTE This traditional West African meat stew, known as *mafé*, is made with vegetables and a peanut and tomato-flavored sauce and typically served with rice.

FLEMISH BEEF STEW

(NF)

PREPARATION TIME:
10 minutes

COOKING TIME:
2 hours 50 minutes

Serves: 4

- 2 tablespoons butter
- 2 lb 4 oz (1 kg) chuck roast (braising steak), cut into 2-inch (5-cm) cubes
- 3 onions, thinly sliced
- 1 tablespoon brown sugar
- 2 tablespoons red wine vinegar
- 3 bay leaves
- 2 cups (16 fl oz/475 ml) ale
- Salt and pepper, to taste
- Hot mustard
- 3 ½ oz (100 g) French gingerbread, sliced
- French fries, to serve

① Melt the butter in a Dutch oven (casserole) over high heat. Add half the meat and lightly brown for 2–3 minutes on each side. Transfer the meat to a plate and set aside. Repeat with the remaining half.

② Add the onions to the pan and sauté for 10–12 minutes over medium heat, until very soft. Sprinkle with the brown sugar and caramelize for 2 minutes. Stir in the vinegar and cook for 5 minutes, until completely reduced.

③ Return the meat to the pan. Add the bay leaves. Pour in the beer, stir, and cover. Season with salt and pepper.

④ Spread the mustard over the gingerbread slices and place them on top of the stew. Cover, bring to a boil, then reduce the heat to low. Simmer for 2½ hours, until the meat is tender. Discard the bay leaves.

⑤ Serve with French fries.

NOTE This dish can be prepared in advance and tastes even better the next day!

BEEF WITH CARROTS

(DF) (NF)

PREPARATION TIME:
15 minutes

COOKING TIME:
1 hour 40 minutes

Serves: 4

2 tablespoons olive oil

2 lb 4 oz (1 kg) chuck roast (braising steak), cut into bite-sized chunks

1 tablespoon all-purpose (plain) flour

12–14 carrots, sliced into thick rounds

2 onions, thinly sliced

2 sprigs thyme

6 ⅓ cups (51 fl oz/1.5 liters) beef stock

Salt and pepper, to taste

Fresh tagliatelle, steamed potatoes, mashed potatoes, or rice, to serve

① Heat the oil in a Dutch oven (casserole) over medium-high heat. Add the meat and brown for 2–3 minutes on each side. Sprinkle in the flour and stir.

② Add the carrots, onions, thyme, and stock. Season with salt and pepper. Bring to a boil. Cover, reduce the heat to low, and simmer for 1½ hours, until the meat is tender.

③ Serve with tagliatelle, steamed potatoes, mashed potatoes, or rice.

QUICK AND EASY CHILI CON CARNE

(DF) (GF) (NF)

PREPARATION TIME:
15 minutes

COOKING TIME:
35 minutes

Serves: 4

- 1 tablespoon olive oil
- 1 onion, thinly sliced
- 1 red bell pepper, seeded, deveined, and cut into strips
- 1 green bell pepper, seeded, deveined, and cut into strips
- 12 oz (350 g) ground (minced) beef
- 1½ tablespoons ground cumin
- 1 generous tablespoon smoked paprika
- ½ teaspoon chili powder
- 1 (14-oz/400-g) can chopped tomatoes
- 9 oz (250 g) canned kidney beans, drained
- 1 tablespoon dried oregano
- Scant 1 cup (7 fl oz/200 ml) beef stock
- Salt and pepper, to taste
- Queso fresco cheese, to serve
- Sour cream, to serve
- Corn tortillas or rice, to serve

① Heat the oil in a Dutch oven (casserole) over medium-high heat. Add the onion, bell peppers, and beef and sauté for 7 minutes, until the moisture evaporates. Add the cumin, paprika, and chili powder and stir for 3 minutes.

② Add the tomatoes, kidney beans, oregano, and stock. Bring to a boil, then reduce the heat to medium-low. Cover and simmer for 25 minutes. Season with salt and pepper.

③ Serve with queso fresco, sour cream, and tortillas or rice.

BEER-BRAISED BEEF STEW

(DF) (NF)

PREPARATION TIME:
20 minutes

COOKING TIME:
1 hour 45 minutes

Serves: 4

- 2 tablespoons olive oil
- 2 lb 4 oz (1 kg) chuck roast (braising steak), cut into bite-sized cubes
- 1 onion, thinly sliced
- 2 cloves garlic, finely chopped
- 1⅓ cups (11 fl oz/330 ml) amber ale
- 1 tablespoon all-purpose (plain) flour
- 2 carrots, cut into chunks
- 1 parsnip, cut into chunks
- 14 oz (400 g) new potatoes, halved
- 2 tablespoons tomato paste (purée)
- 2 teaspoons sweet paprika
- 1⅔ cups (14 fl oz/400 ml) beef stock
- 1 bouquet garni
- ½ winter squash, such as red kuri, or pumpkin, peeled and finely chopped (see Note)
- Salt and pepper, to taste

① Heat the oil in a Dutch oven (casserole) over high heat. Add the beef and brown for 3–4 minutes on each side. Transfer the meat to a plate.

② To the same pan, add the onion and garlic and sauté for 3–5 minutes. Add ⅓ cup (3 fl oz/90 ml) of the ale, scraping up the brown bits from the bottom of the pan with a wooden spoon. Cook until the liquid is reduced by half.

③ Dust the meat with the flour, then return it to the pan. Add the carrots, parsnip, potatoes, tomato paste (purée), and paprika. Pour in the stock and the remaining 1 cup (8 fl oz/250 ml) of ale and stir. Bring to a boil, then reduce the heat to low and add the bouquet garni. Cover and simmer for 1 hour.

④ Add the squash (or pumpkin), cover, and cook for another 30 minutes. Season with salt and pepper. Discard the bouquet garni.

⑤ Serve hot.

NOTE Because red kuri squash has thin skin, it can be left unpeeled unless its texture is undesirable.

CREAMY BEEF WITH POTATOES

(GF) (NF)

PREPARATION TIME:
10 minutes

COOKING TIME:
35 minutes

Serves: 4

2 tablespoons olive oil

4 potatoes, cut into large chunks

1 onion, thinly sliced

12 oz (350 g) ground (minced) beef

3 tablespoons crème fraîche

Salt and pepper, to taste

2–4 eggs

1. Heat the oil in a Dutch oven (casserole) over medium heat. Add the potatoes and onion and sauté for 5 minutes.
2. Add the beef and cover with 2 cups (16 fl oz/475 ml) of cold water. Bring to a boil, cover, and simmer over medium-low heat for 25 minutes, stirring occasionally, until the water has been entirely absorbed.
3. Stir in the crème fraîche. Season with salt and pepper.
4. Crack the eggs into the pan and cook, untouched, for another 5 minutes. Season with salt and pepper.
5. Serve hot.

HUNGARIAN GOULASH

PREPARATION TIME:
20 minutes

COOKING TIME:
2 hours

Serves: 6

- 3 tablespoons sunflower oil
- 3 lb 5 oz (1.5 kg) chuck roast (braising steak), cut into ¾-inch (2-cm) cubes
- 2–3 onions, thinly sliced
- 1 cup (8 fl oz/250 ml) strong vegetable stock
- 2 tablespoons sweet paprika
- 1 teaspoon smoked paprika (optional)
- ¼ teaspoon chili powder
- 1 generous teaspoon ground caraway or ½ teaspoon caraway seeds
- 2 potatoes, cut into chunks
- 2 red bell peppers, seeded, deveined, and cut into strips
- Salt and pepper, to taste

① Heat 2 tablespoons of oil in a large skillet over high heat. Working in batches, add the meat and brown for 2–3 minutes on each side. Transfer to a Dutch oven (casserole).

② Heat the remaining tablespoon of oil in the same skillet over medium-high heat. Add the onions and sauté for 5 minutes. Pour in stock and scrape the brown bits from the bottom of the pan to dissolve the caramelized juices. Pour the mixture into the Dutch oven. Add the sweet paprika, smoked paprika, if using, chili powder, and caraway.

③ Bring the mixture to a boil, then reduce the heat to medium-low. Cover and gently simmer for 1 hour 20 minutes. If the mixture appears dry, add more water to the pan.

④ Add the potatoes and bell peppers and simmer for another 30 minutes. Season with salt and pepper.

⑤ Serve hot.

LASAGNA CASSEROLE

(NF)

PREPARATION TIME:
10 minutes

COOKING TIME:
25 minutes

Serves: 4

1 onion, thinly sliced	3 ½ oz (100 g) mascarpone cheese
4 tablespoons olive oil	2 cups (16 fl oz/475 ml) puréed tomatoes (passata)
6 sheets lasagna noodles	Salt and pepper, to taste
10 ½ oz (300 g) ground (minced) beef	3 ½ oz (100 g) ricotta cheese, crumbled
2 cloves garlic, chopped	2 tablespoons chopped basil
1 tablespoon dried oregano	½ cup (1 ¾ oz/50 g) grated Parmesan, plus extra to serve
1 ¾ cups (7 oz/200 g) shredded mozzarella	

① Put the onion in a 9-inch (23-cm) Dutch oven (casserole) and drizzle with 2 tablespoons of oil. Cover with 2 lasagna sheets, then add half the ground (minced) beef, garlic, oregano, mozzarella, and mascarpone. Pour in ¾ cup of the puréed tomatoes (passata), then season with salt and pepper. Repeat the process and finish with 2 lasagna noodles.

② Pour in the remaining 1¼ cups of puréed tomatoes and add the ricotta. Sprinkle with basil and Parmesan. Season with salt and pepper. Drizzle with the remaining 2 tablespoons of oil. Cover and cook over low heat for 25 minutes.

③ Serve with grated Parmesan.

BEEF HOT POT

PREPARATION TIME:
30 minutes, plus 12 hours marinating time

COOKING TIME:
3 hours

Serves: 6

3 lb 5 oz (1.5 kg) beef, cut into bite-sized cubes (see Note)

4 onions, thinly sliced

2 carrots, sliced into rounds

2 leeks, white part only, sliced

1 rib celery, sliced

5 juniper berries

1 bouquet garni

3 cups (25 fl oz/750 ml) Riesling wine

8–10 waxy potatoes, sliced into thin rounds (3 lb 5 oz/1.5 kg)

Salt and pepper, to taste

2 ½ cups (10 ½ oz/300 g) all-purpose (plain) flour

① In a large bowl, combine the meat, half the onions, carrots, leeks, and celery. Add the juniper berries and bouquet garni. Pour in the wine and stir to combine. Cover and refrigerate for 12 hours to marinate.

② Drain the marinated meat and vegetables through a fine-mesh strainer, reserving the marinade.

③ In the bottom of an oval Dutch oven (casserole), arrange a layer of potatoes. Sprinkle over the remaining onions, then cover with a layer of marinated meat and vegetables. Season with salt and pepper. Repeat the layering process, finishing with a layer of potatoes. Pour over the reserved marinade.

④ Preheat the oven to 350°F (180°C/Gas mark 4).

⑤ In a bowl, combine the flour and ½ cup (4 fl oz/120 ml) of water. Mix well. Roll the dough into a sausage shape and press it around the lid of the Dutch oven to form an airtight seal. Bake for 3 hours, until the meat is tender.

⑥ Serve hot.

NOTE The beef can be replaced with a combination of beef, lamb, and pork.

PROVENÇAL BEEF STEW

(DF) (NF)

PREPARATION TIME:
15 minutes, plus 3–12 hours marinating time

COOKING TIME:
2 hours 50 minutes

Serves: 6

- 2 lb 12 oz (1.2 kg) blade steak, cut into 1½-inch (4-cm) chunks
- 3 cups (25 fl oz/750 ml) red wine
- 2 tablespoons olive oil
- 1 onion, thinly sliced
- 2 cloves garlic, chopped
- 10 rashers bacon, sliced
- 1 tablespoon all-purpose (plain) flour
- 2–3 sprigs thyme
- 1 bay leaf
- Scant 1 cup (7 fl oz/200 ml) beef stock
- 2 zucchinis (courgettes), thinly sliced into rounds
- Salt and pepper, to taste
- Steamed potatoes or rice, to serve

① In a large bowl, combine the steak and wine and cover. Refrigerate for at least 3 hours or overnight.

② Heat the oil in a Dutch oven (casserole) over medium heat. Add the onion and garlic and sauté for 5 minutes, until softened. Add the bacon and cook for 3–5 minutes, until golden brown. Transfer to a bowl and set aside.

③ Heat the same pan over high heat. Using a slotted spoon, remove the steak from the marinade and transfer it to the hot pan. Brown for 2–3 minutes on each side. Stir in the flour and cook for 2 minutes.

④ Add the bacon mixture, thyme, and bay leaf. Pour in the reserved wine marinate and stock. Bring to a boil, then reduce the heat to low. Cover and simmer for 1½ hours, stirring occasionally.

⑤ Add the zucchinis (courgettes), cover, and cook for another 30 minutes. Uncover and cook for another 20–30 minutes over medium heat to lightly reduce the sauce. Discard the bay leaf. Season with salt and pepper.

⑥ Serve with steamed potatoes or rice.

VARIATION
You can replace the zucchinis with carrots.

BEEF BIRYANI

(GF) (NF)

PREPARATION TIME:
15 minutes, plus 3–12 hours marinating time

COOKING TIME:
40 minutes

Serves: 4

FOR THE MARINATED BEEF:

4 cloves garlic, chopped

½ cup (1 oz/30 g) chopped cilantro (coriander), plus extra for garnish

⅓ cup (¾ oz/20 g) chopped mint, plus extra for garnish

1 tablespoon grated ginger

1 tablespoon ground coriander

1 tablespoon ground turmeric

1 teaspoon ground cumin

¼ cup (2 oz/55 g) plain yogurt

Salt and pepper, to taste

1 lb 12 oz (800 g) round steak, cut into cubes

FOR THE BIRYANI:

2 tablespoons olive oil

2 onions, thinly sliced

1½ cups (10½ oz/300 g) basmati rice, rinsed thoroughly and drained

¾ cup (3½ oz/100 g) fresh or frozen peas

1 teaspoon ground cinnamon

1 teaspoon ground turmeric

Salt and pepper, to taste

① Prepare the marinated beef. Combine all the ingredients except the beef in a large bowl. Add the beef and mix until well coated. Cover and refrigerate for at least 3 hours or, ideally, overnight to marinate.

② Make the biryani. Heat the oil in a Dutch oven (casserole) over medium-high heat. Add the onions and sauté for 7 minutes, until softened. Transfer to a plate and set aside to use later as a garnish.

③ To the same pan, add the beef with its marinade, the rice, peas, cinnamon, and turmeric. Pour in enough water to cover and bring to a boil. Reduce the heat to low, then cover and simmer for 30 minutes. Season with salt and pepper.

④ Garnish with the fried onions, cilantro (coriander), and mint leaves. Serve hot.

VARIATION

The peas may be replaced with diced zucchinis (courgettes) or bell peppers.

OSSO BUCO

PREPARATION TIME:
15 minutes

COOKING TIME:
1 hour 15 minutes

Serves: 6

- 4 tomatoes (1 lb 2 oz/500 g)
- 5 tablespoons olive oil
- 2 onions, thinly sliced
- 1 clove garlic, chopped
- 1 rib celery, thinly sliced
- 6 (7-oz/200-g) veal shanks (see Note)
- 2 tablespoons all-purpose flour
- 1 bay leaf
- Scant 1 cup (7 fl oz/200 ml) dry white wine
- Salt and pepper, to taste
- 6 cups (47 fl oz/1.4 liters) vegetable or chicken stock
- Sprig of rosemary, leaves only, chopped
- 2 tablespoons chopped parsley, plus extra for garnish

① Preheat the oven to 400°F (200°C/Gas mark 6).

② Bring a large saucepan of water to a boil. Make a small "X" at the bottom of each tomato, then carefully add them to the boiling water. Blanch for 1 minute, until the skins begin to loosen. Transfer the tomatoes immediately to a bowl of ice water to cool. Once cooled, peel off the skins starting at the X, then seed and chop the tomatoes.

③ Heat the oil in a Dutch oven (casserole) over medium-high heat. Add the onions, garlic, celery, and tomatoes and sauté for 6 minutes, until the onions are softened.

④ Lightly dredge the veal shanks in flour. Add them to the pan and brown for 3 minutes on each side. Add the bay leaf and wine and simmer over low heat until the liquid is reduced by a third. Season with salt and pepper.

⑤ Pour in the stock and bring to a boil. Cover with an ovenproof lid and bake for 1 hour, until the veal is fork tender.

⑥ Remove the veal shanks and set aside. Add the rosemary and parsley to the pan and simmer over medium heat until the liquid is reduced by half. Return the veal to the pan. Discard the bay leaf. Season with salt and pepper, then sprinkle with parsley.

⑦ Serve hot.

NOTE The best osso buco is made from hind shanks, which provide the most tender and flavorful meat. Scoop out the rich marrow in the veal shank with a small fork and enjoy!

VEAL BLANQUETTE

(NF)

PREPARATION TIME:
20 minutes

COOKING TIME:
1 hour 50 minutes

Serves: 4

- 1 lb 12 oz (800 g) veal chuck, neck, or shank, trimmed and cut into chunks
- 3 carrots, sliced into rounds (10 ½ oz/300 g)
- 2 leeks, white part only, sliced into 1 ¼-inch (3-cm) segments
- 1 onion, studded with 3 whole cloves
- 1 bouquet garni
- ½ cup (1 stick) butter
- 9 oz (250 g) button mushrooms, sliced
- ⅓ cup (2 oz/60 g) all-purpose (plain) flour
- 2 egg yolks
- Scant 1 cup (7 fl oz/200 ml) crème fraîche
- Juice of 1 lemon (optional)
- Salt and pepper, to taste
- Rice, to serve

① Place the veal in a Dutch oven (casserole). Cover with boiling water and bring to a gentle boil. Add the carrots, leeks, onion, and bouquet garni. Cover, reduce the heat to medium-low, and simmer for 1½ hours. Discard the bouquet garni.

② Melt 2 tablespoons of butter in a skillet over medium heat. Add the mushrooms and sauté for 5 minutes. Set aside.

③ Melt the remaining 6 tablespoons of butter in a small saucepan over medium heat. Whisk in the flour and cook for 3 minutes, until nutty and golden. Add a ladle of the cooking liquid from the veal and simmer for 2–3 minutes.

④ In a bowl, whisk the egg yolks, crème fraîche, and lemon juice, if using. Stir the mixture into the Dutch oven, then add the roux and mushrooms. Cook for 5 minutes over low heat. Season with salt and pepper.

⑤ Serve with rice.

VEAL AND CHORIZO BEAN STEW

(DF) (GF) (NF)

PREPARATION TIME:
15 minutes

COOKING TIME:
2 hours 25 minutes

Serves: 4

- 2 tablespoons olive oil
- 1 onion, thinly sliced
- 1 lb 2 oz (500 g) braising veal, such as chuck, neck, or brisket, cut into chunks
- 2 ¾ oz (80 g) chorizo, sliced
- 2 carrots, cut in half lengthwise and cut into ¾-inch (2-cm) thick half moons
- 1 clove garlic, chopped
- 2 tablespoons tomato paste (purée)
- 1 bouquet garni
- 1 lb 12 oz (800 g) canned white beans in tomato sauce
- Salt and pepper, to taste

① Heat the oil in a Dutch oven (casserole) over medium-high heat. Add the onion and sauté for 7 minutes. Add the veal, then brown for 2–3 minutes on each side.

② Stir in the chorizo, carrots, and garlic, then add the tomato paste (purée), bouquet garni, and ½ cup (4 fl oz/120 ml) of water. Bring to a boil, then reduce the heat to medium-low. Cover and simmer for 2 hours, stirring occasionally.

③ Add the beans and cook for another 5–10 minutes. Discard the bouquet garni. Season with salt and pepper.

④ Serve hot.

VEAL AND MUSHROOM TAGLIATELLE

(NF)

PREPARATION TIME:
10 minutes

COOKING TIME:
30 minutes

Serves: 4

2 tablespoons olive oil

12 oz (350 g) assorted mushrooms, cleaned and thinly sliced

1 onion, thinly sliced

1 (12-oz/350-g) piece veal, cut into thin strips

12 oz (350 g) dried egg tagliatelle

5 ½ oz (150 g) garlic and herb cheese spread, such as Boursin®

3 ½ cups (27 fl oz/800 ml) beef stock

Pepper, to taste

4 tablespoons chopped parsley

4 tablespoons chopped chives

① Heat the oil in a Dutch oven (casserole) over high heat. Add the mushrooms and sauté for 3 minutes. Add the onion and veal and cook for another 3 minutes.

② Stir in the pasta, cheese spread, and stock. Bring to a boil. Cover and cook over medium heat for 20 minutes, stirring occasionally. Set aside to rest for 2 minutes. Season with pepper.

③ Sprinkle with parsley and chives, then serve.

CREAMY VEAL AND VEGETABLE STEW

(GF) (NF)

PREPARATION TIME:
20 minutes

COOKING TIME:
1 hour 50 minutes

Serves: 4

Olive oil, for frying

1 lb 12 oz (800 g) veal chuck, cut into 1½-inch (4-cm) cubes

2 shallots, thinly sliced

2 cloves garlic, chopped

Scant 1 cup (7 fl oz/200 ml) dry white wine

2 carrots, sliced into thin rounds

2 turnips, chopped

1 bay leaf

1⅔ cups (14 fl oz/400 ml) chicken stock

3–4 potatoes, cut into chunks (1 lb 5 oz/600 g)

Scant 1 cup (7 fl oz/200 ml) light (single) cream

1 tablespoon cornstarch (cornflour)

1 tablespoon mustard

7 oz (200 g) cremini mushrooms, thinly sliced

Salt and pepper, to taste

① Heat the oil in a Dutch oven (casserole) over medium-high heat. Add the veal and sear on each side for 2–3 minutes. Remove the meat.

② To the same pan, add the shallots and garlic and sauté for 3–5 minutes, until softened. Deglaze with the wine and reduce the liquid by half. Return the meat to the pan, then add the carrots, turnips, and bay leaf. Pour in the stock and bring to a boil. Reduce the heat to medium-low, cover, and simmer for 1 hour.

③ Add the potatoes and cook for another 20 minutes. Stir in the cream, cornstarch (cornflour), mustard, and mushrooms. Cook for 15 minutes uncovered. Discard the bay leaf.

④ Season with salt and pepper. Serve hot.

BRAISED VEAL WITH CARROTS AND WALNUTS

(GF)

PREPARATION TIME:
20 minutes

COOKING TIME:
1 hour 10 minutes

Serves: 4

1 tablespoon sunflower oil or 2 tablespoons lard

2 lb 4 oz (1 kg) milk-fed veal roast, preferably top round or sirloin

1 onion, thinly sliced

2 shallots, thinly sliced

2 carrots, diced

Scant 1 cup (7 fl oz/200 ml) dry white wine

1 bouquet garni

Salt and pepper, to taste

5 cremini mushrooms, thinly sliced (optional)

¾ cup (3 ½ oz/100 g) walnuts, coarsely chopped

⅔ cup (5 fl oz/150 ml) crème fraîche

Fresh pasta or rice, to serve

① Heat the oil (or lard) in a Dutch oven (casserole) over medium-high heat. Add the veal and sear on each side for 2–3 minutes. Remove the meat.

② Add the onion, shallots, and carrots and sauté for 2 minutes. Return the veal to the pan, then add the wine and bouquet garni. Season with salt and pepper. Cover and simmer over medium-low heat for 1 hour, turning occasionally. Discard the bouquet garni.

③ Add the mushrooms, if using, walnuts, and crème fraîche. Bring to a boil, then season again. Remove the veal, slice, and plate.

④ Ladle the veal in the walnut sauce and serve with fresh pasta or rice.

BEER-BRAISED VEAL ROULADES

(NF)

PREPARATION TIME:
10 minutes

COOKING TIME:
1 hour–1 hour 15 minutes

Serves: 4

1½ tablespoons butter

2 shallots, finely chopped

4 veal roulades (paupiettes)

1⅓ cups (11 oz/330 ml) amber ale

2 apples, peeled, cored, and diced into ½-inch (1-cm) cubes

4 Belgian spice cookies (speculoos), coarsely crumbled

Salt and pepper

1 tablespoon cornstarch (cornflour)

Mashed potatoes or fresh pasta, to serve

① Melt the butter in a Dutch oven (casserole) over medium-high heat. Add the shallots and sauté for 3 minutes. Transfer to a bowl, then set aside.

② Add the veal and sear on each side for 2–3 minutes. Return the shallots to the pan, then add the beer and bring to a boil.

③ Add the apples and cookies (biscuits). Cover, then simmer over medium-low heat for 45 minutes–1 hour, occasionally basting the roulades with the cooking juices. Season with salt and pepper.

④ Dissolve the cornstarch (cornflour) in a ladle of sauce from the pan. Add this mixture to the sauce and cook for a few minutes over low heat until thickened.

⑤ Serve with mashed potatoes or pasta.

VEAL MARENGO

(DF) (GF) (NF)

PREPARATION TIME:
15 minutes

COOKING TIME:
1 hour 25 minutes

Serves: 4

Olive oil, for frying

1 lb 12 oz (800 g) veal shank, cut into 1½-inch (4-cm) cubes

2 shallots, chopped

3 cloves garlic, minced

3 carrots, sliced

Scant ½ cup (3½ fl oz/100 ml) dry white wine

1 (14-oz/400-g) can chopped tomatoes

1 tablespoon tomato paste (purée)

Salt and pepper, to taste

9 oz (250 g) button mushrooms, sliced

Chopped parsley

Fresh pasta or rice, to serve

① Heat the oil in a Dutch oven (casserole) over medium-high heat. Add the veal and sear on each side for 2–3 minutes. Remove the meat and set aside.

② To the same pan, add the shallots and garlic and sauté for 3 minutes, until softened. Add the carrots and wine and cook until the liquid is reduced by half. Add the veal.

③ Add the tomatoes and tomato paste. Pour in 1¼ cups (10 fl oz/300 ml) of water and bring to a boil. Reduce the heat to low, cover, and simmer for 1 hour. Season with salt and pepper.

④ Add the mushrooms and cook for another 15 minutes.

⑤ Sprinkle with parsley and serve hot with fresh pasta or rice.

BASQUE-STYLE VEAL STEW

PREPARATION TIME:
10 minutes

COOKING TIME:
45 minutes

Serves: 4

- 2 tablespoons olive oil
- 1 lb 12 oz (800 g) veal neck or chuck, cut into small cubes
- 2 onions, thinly sliced
- 2 cloves garlic, chopped
- 6 mild sweet peppers, such as Doux des Landes or Cubanelle, seeded, deveined, and finely chopped
- 2 red bell peppers, seeded, deveined, and finely chopped
- 1 tablespoon Espelette powder
- Scant ½ cup (3 ½ fl oz/100 ml) dry white wine
- 100 g (3 ½ oz) cured ham, cut into small cubes
- 2 cups (16 fl oz/475 ml) veal stock
- Salt and pepper
- Sautéed potatoes or rice, to serve

① Heat the oil in a Dutch oven (casserole) over medium-high heat. Add the veal and sear on each side for 2–3 minutes. Remove the meat and set aside.

② To the same pan, add the onions, garlic, both types of peppers, and Espelette pepper. Cook for 5 minutes over medium heat.

③ Deglaze with the wine, scraping up the brown bits from the bottom of the pan with a wooden spoon. Add the veal, ham, and stock. Season with salt and pepper. Stir, cover, and cook for 30 minutes. Stir the mixture twice during cooking, but no more than this in order to retain as much steam as possible.

④ Serve hot with sautéed potatoes or rice.

NOTE Veal *axoa* is a traditional Basque stew, often highlighted by the mild heat of Espelette pepper. Known for its rustic simplicity, this dish showcases the bold, earthy flavors of Basque cuisine.

FLEMISH VEAL STEW

(NF)

PREPARATION TIME:
20 minutes

COOKING TIME:
1 hour 30 minutes

Serves: 4

- 1 tablespoon olive oil
- 1 lb 12 oz (800 g) veal chuck, cut into chunks
- 1 onion, thinly sliced
- 1 clove garlic, chopped
- 2 tablespoons all-purpose (plain) flour
- 1⅓ cups (11 oz/330 ml) lager
- Sprig of thyme
- 2 bay leaves
- Salt and pepper
- 9 oz (250 g) button mushrooms, very finely sliced
- Scant ½ cup (3½ fl oz/100 ml) whipping cream
- Fresh pasta, French fries, or rice, to serve

① Heat the oil in a Dutch oven (casserole) over high heat. Add the veal pieces and sear on all sides for 5 minutes in total. Set aside.

② Add the onion and garlic to the pan and sauté for 3 minutes. Return the veal to the pan, sprinkle with the flour, and mix well.

③ Add the beer, thyme, and bay leaves. Season with salt and pepper. Bring to a boil, then reduce the heat to low. Cover and simmer gently for 1 hour, stirring occasionally.

④ Add the mushrooms and cream and cook for another 20 minutes. Discard the thyme and bay leaves.

⑤ Serve with fresh pasta, French fries, or rice.

COCONUT-MANGO VEAL CURRY

(DF) (GF) (NF)

PREPARATION TIME:
20 minutes

COOKING TIME:
50 minutes

Serves: 4

- 2 tablespoons sunflower oil
- 1 onion, thinly sliced
- 1 lb 5 oz (600 g) veal knuckle, cut into chunks
- 1 red bell pepper, seeded, deveined, and sliced
- 1 green bell pepper, seeded, deveined, and sliced
- 1 cup (8 fl oz/250 ml) coconut milk
- 1 tablespoon curry powder
- 1 mango, stoned and diced
- Cilantro (coriander), for garnish
- Jasmine rice, to serve

① Heat the oil in a Dutch oven (casserole) over medium-high heat. Add the onion and sauté for 7 minutes, until softened. Add the veal and peppers and sauté for 5 minutes.

② Pour in the coconut milk and add the curry powder. Cover, reduce the heat to low, and simmer for 30 minutes. Add the mango and cook for another 5 minutes.

③ Garnish with cilantro (coriander). Serve hot with rice.

LAMB

MOROCCAN LAMB AND CHICKPEA CHORBA	186
LAMB TIKKA MASALA	188
LAMB KOFTA AND FAVA BEAN TAGINE	190
HERBED LAMB WITH POTATOES AND PEAS	192
LAMB NAVARIN	194
SLOW-BRAISED LEG OF LAMB	196
CIDER-BRAISED LAMB SHANKS	198
LAMB SHANKS WITH GARLIC AND THYME	200

MOROCCAN LAMB AND CHICKPEA CHORBA

DF NF

PREPARATION TIME:
15 minutes

COOKING TIME:
55 minutes

Serves: 4

- 2 tablespoons olive oil
- 1 onion, thinly sliced
- 2 cloves garlic, chopped
- 10 ½ oz (300 g) lamb shoulder, cut into large cubes
- 1 teaspoon ground turmeric
- 1 teaspoon paprika
- 1 teaspoon ras el hanout
- ½ teaspoon ground ginger
- 3 tomatoes, diced
- 1 zucchini (courgette), diced
- 1 red bell pepper, seeded, deveined, and cut into strips
- ½ cup (2 ½ oz/70 g) tomato paste (purée)
- 4 sprigs cilantro (coriander), chopped
- Sprig of mint, chopped
- ¾ cup (2 ¾ oz/80 g) short vermicelli pasta
- Generous 1 cup (7 oz/200 g) drained canned chickpeas
- Salt and pepper, to taste

① Heat the oil in a Dutch oven (casserole) over medium-high heat. Add the onion and sauté for 5 minutes. Add the garlic, lamb, spices, tomatoes, zucchini (courgette), and bell pepper. Sauté for 5 minutes.

② Add the tomato paste (purée), cilantro (coriander), and mint. Pour in 4¼ cups (34 fl oz/1 liter) of water. Bring to a boil, then reduce the heat to low. Cover and simmer for 40 minutes.

③ Add the vermicelli and chickpeas. Cover and cook for another 10 minutes. Season with salt and pepper and serve hot.

NOTE Chorba is a popular African soup often served during Ramadan.

LAMB TIKKA MASALA

(GF) (NF)

PREPARATION TIME:
10 minutes, plus 1 hour marinating time

COOKING TIME:
35 minutes

Serves: 4

FOR THE MARINATED LAMB:

¼ cup (2 fl oz/60 ml) plain yogurt

1 tablespoon garam masala

1 teaspoon ground cumin

1 teaspoon ground turmeric

1 lb 5 oz (600 g) lamb shoulder, cut into cubes

FOR THE TIKKA MASALA:

2 tablespoons neutral oil, such as canola (rapeseed) oil

1 onion, thinly sliced

3 carrots, sliced into thin rounds

2 cloves garlic, chopped

1 cup (5 ½ oz/150 g) fresh or frozen peas

1 tablespoon grated ginger

Scant 1 cup (7 fl oz/200 ml) coconut milk

1 (14-oz/400-g) can chopped tomatoes

Salt, to taste

Rice, semolina, or bulgur, to serve

① Make the marinated lamb. Combine all the ingredients except the lamb in a large bowl. Add the lamb, mix to coat, and refrigerate for 1 hour.

② Make the tikka masala. Heat the oil in a Dutch oven (casserole) over medium-high heat. Add the onion and sauté for 3 minutes. Add the carrots, garlic, peas, and ginger.

③ Stir in the coconut milk and tomatoes. Bring to a boil, then reduce the heat to low. Cover and cook for 10 minutes.

④ Add the lamb and its marinade, cover, and cook for 20 minutes, until tender. Season with salt.

⑤ Serve hot with rice, semolina, or bulgur.

LAMB KOFTA AND FAVA BEAN TAGINE

(DF) (GF) (NF)

PREPARATION TIME:
15 minutes

COOKING TIME:
50 minutes

Serves: 4

FOR THE TAGINE:

2 tablespoons olive oil

1 red onion, thinly sliced

1 teaspoon ground turmeric

1 teaspoon paprika

4 tablespoons tomato paste (purée)

1⅓ cups (14 oz/400 g) fresh or frozen fava (broad) beans

3 tomatoes, chopped

1 tablespoon chopped parsley, plus extra for garnish

Salt and pepper, to taste

Bread, to serve

FOR THE KOFTAS:

1 lb 2 oz (500 g) ground lamb

1 teaspoon ground turmeric

1 teaspoon paprika

2 tablespoons chopped parsley

Salt and pepper

① Prepare the tagine. Heat the oil in a Dutch oven (casserole) over medium-high heat. Add the onion and sauté for 7 minutes, until softened. Stir in the turmeric and paprika, then add the tomato paste (purée) and a scant ½ cup (3½ fl oz/100 ml) of water. Cook for 2–3 minutes.

② Add the fava (broad) beans, tomatoes, and parsley, then add enough water to cover the contents. Mix, cover, and simmer over medium-low heat for 30 minutes. Season with salt and pepper.

③ Meanwhile, prepare the koftas. Combine all the ingredients in a large bowl and mix well. With slightly moistened hands, shape the mixture into meatballs about 1½ inches (4 cm) in diameter.

④ Add the koftas to the pan and cook over medium heat for 10 minutes, until cooked through.

⑤ Sprinkle with parsley and serve hot with bread.

HERBED LAMB WITH POTATOES AND PEAS

PREPARATION TIME:
15 minutes

COOKING TIME:
1 hour

Serves: 4

2 tablespoons olive oil

1 lb 12 oz (800 g) lamb shoulder, cut into large cubes

1 onion, thinly sliced

1 tablespoon apple cider vinegar

1 tablespoon herbes de Provence

Salt and pepper, to taste

1 lb 5 oz (600 g) fingerling potatoes, cut larger ones in half

1½ cups (7 oz/200 g) fresh or frozen peas

① Heat the oil in a Dutch oven (casserole) over medium-high heat. Add the lamb and brown on all sides for 7 minutes total. Add the onion and sauté for 5 minutes.

② Add the vinegar and herbes de Provence, then season with salt and pepper. Add 1 cup (8 fl oz/250 ml) of cold water. Bring to a boil, then reduce the heat to medium-low. Cover and simmer for 30 minutes.

③ Add the potatoes and cook for 15 minutes, until tender. If the mixture appears dry, top up with hot water.

④ Add the peas and cook for another 5 minutes.

⑤ Serve hot.

LAMB NAVARIN

(NF)

PREPARATION TIME:
25 minutes

COOKING TIME:
1 hour

Serves: 4–6

- 2 tablespoons sunflower oil
- 2 lb 12 oz (1.2 kg) lamb shoulder, cut into large chunks, and neck, sliced
- 1 tablespoon all-purpose (plain) flour
- Salt and pepper, to taste
- Grated nutmeg, to taste
- ½ cup (3½ oz/100 g) canned chopped tomatoes
- 2 cloves garlic, chopped
- 1 bouquet garni
- 2 tablespoons butter
- 2 bunches spring carrots
- 1–2 turnips, cut into chunks
- Bunch of scallions (spring onions)
- 2¼ cups (10½ oz/300 g) peas
- 10½ oz (300 g) green beans

① Heat the oil in a large Dutch oven (casserole) over medium-high heat. Add the lamb shoulder and neck and brown on all sides for 7–10 minutes in total. Sprinkle with the flour and mix well. Cook for 3 minutes, stirring constantly. Season with salt, pepper, and grated nutmeg.

② Add the tomatoes, garlic, and bouquet garni. Pour in enough water to cover the contents. Bring to a boil, then reduce the heat to medium-low. Cover and simmer for 25 minutes.

③ Melt the butter in a high-sided skillet over medium-high heat. Add the carrots, turnips, and onions and sauté for 7 minutes. Transfer this mixture to the pan.

④ Add the peas and mix well. Reduce the heat to low and cook for 10 minutes.

⑤ Meanwhile, bring a saucepan of water to a boil. Add the green beans and boil for 2–3 minutes. Blanch in a large bowl of ice water. Add the green beans to the stew and cook for another 5 minutes. Discard the bouquet garni. Season with salt and pepper.

⑥ Serve hot.

SLOW-BRAISED LEG OF LAMB

(GF) (NF)

PREPARATION TIME:
10 minutes

COOKING TIME:
7 hours 10 minutes

Serves: 6

1 (4-lb/1.8-kg) leg of lamb	1¼ cups (10 fl oz/300 ml) dry white wine
Salt and pepper, to taste	2½ cups (20 fl oz/600 ml) vegetable stock
3½ tablespoons butter	1 bouquet garni (see Tip)
2 onions, thinly sliced	Roast potatoes or a green vegetable, such as asparagus or green beans, to serve
4 cloves garlic, chopped	

① Preheat the oven to 250°F (120°C/Gas mark ½). Season the lamb with salt and pepper.

② Melt the butter in a Dutch oven (casserole) over medium-high heat. Add the lamb and brown for 7–10 minutes. Add the onions and garlic.

③ Pour in the wine and deglaze. Add the stock and bouquet garni. Bring to a boil. Cover and cook in the oven for 7 hours. Baste the lamb with cooking liquid every 2 hours.

④ Serve hot with roast potatoes or vegetables.

TIP You can also add a few crushed coriander seeds and a quartered lemon with the bouquet garni.

CIDER-BRAISED LAMB SHANKS

(DF) (GF) (NF)

PREPARATION TIME:
10 minutes

COOKING TIME:
1 hour 50 minutes

Serves: 4

- 2 tablespoons sunflower oil
- 4 lamb shanks
- 1 onion, thinly sliced
- 3 cups (25 fl oz/750 ml) hard cider
- 4 tablespoons honey
- 1 teaspoon ground cinnamon
- Salt and pepper, to taste
- 4 sprigs thyme
- 1 tablespoon cornstarch (cornflour), dissolved in 2 tablespoons water
- Carrot or sweet potato purée or vegetable flan, to serve

1. Preheat the oven to 350°F (180°C/Gas mark 4).
2. Heat the oil in a Dutch oven (casserole) over medium-high heat. Add the shanks and sear on all sides. Transfer to a plate and set aside.
3. Add the onion and sauté for 7 minutes, until softened and translucent. Add the cider, honey, and cinnamon. Season with salt and pepper. Bring to a boil.
4. Return the shanks to the pan and add the thyme. Cover and cook in the oven for 1½ hours, basting halfway, until the meat falls off the bone. Discard the thyme.
5. Combine the cornstarch (cornflour) mixture with a ladle of sauce from the pan. Add the mixture to the pan and cook for 3 minutes over medium-high heat until thickened.
6. Serve the lamb shanks with the sauce alongside carrot or sweet potato purée or vegetable flan.

LAMB SHANKS WITH GARLIC AND THYME

(DF) (GF) (NF)

PREPARATION TIME:
15 minutes

COOKING TIME:
1 hour

Serves: 6

- 2 tablespoons olive oil
- 6 lamb shanks
- 4 onions, thinly sliced
- 2 sprigs thyme
- 1–2 teaspoons cumin seeds, crushed
- 1 teaspoon coriander seeds, crushed
- Salt and pepper, to taste
- 4 cloves garlic, crushed
- Mashed potatoes or carrot or broccoli purée, to serve (optional)

① Heat the oil in a Dutch oven (casserole) over medium-high heat. Add the shanks and sear on all sides. Transfer to a plate and set aside.

② Add the onions and sauté for 7 minutes, until softened and translucent. Add the thyme, cumin seeds, and coriander seeds.

③ Return the shanks to the pan, then season with salt and pepper. Add the garlic. Pour in 2 cups (16 fl oz/475 ml) of cold water and bring to a boil. Cover, then reduce the heat to low, and simmer for 20 minutes. Remove the lid and cook for another 25–30 minutes, until the sauce is reduced.

④ Serve hot with mashed potatoes or a carrot or broccoli purée, if using.

SNACKS AND SWEET TREATS

POPCORN	204
EASY BREAD	206
YOGURT CAKE	208
ONE-POT BRIOCHE	210
PEAR AND ALMOND CAKE	212
STEWED PINEAPPLE WITH VANILLA	214
BAKED APPLES WITH COOKIE CRUMB	216
RICE PUDDING	218

POPCORN

(VG) (V) (DF) (GF) (NF) (-5) (-30)

PREPARATION TIME:
5 minutes

COOKING TIME:
5 minutes

Serves: 4

FOR THE POPCORN:

2 tablespoons neutral oil, such as canola (rapeseed) oil

½ cup (3½ oz/100 g) popcorn kernels

FOR A SWEET OPTION:

¼ cup (1¾ oz/50 g) sugar

FOR A SAVORY OPTION:

1 teaspoon salt

1 tablespoon spices of your choice, such as curry powder, paprika, or tandoori spice mix

① Heat the oil in a Dutch oven (casserole) over medium heat. Add the popcorn kernels and stir to coat each kernel with oil. Ensure the kernels are spread in a single layer across the bottom of the pan. If necessary, cook in batches. As soon as the first kernel pops, cover the pan and let the corn pop. Shake the pan occasionally. Stop cooking when there's 2–3 seconds between pops.

② For a sweet popcorn, sprinkle the sugar over the hot popcorn and stir to combine. For the savory version, remove the pan from the heat and add the salt and spices. Stir to combine.

③ Serve.

EASY BREAD

(VG) (V) (DF) (NF) (-S)

PREPARATION TIME:
15 minutes, plus 2 hours
30 minutes resting time

COOKING TIME:
40 minutes

Makes: 1 loaf

4 cups (1 lb 2 oz/500 g) bread flour, plus extra for dusting

1 (¼-oz/8-g) envelope active dry yeast

1½ teaspoons salt

① In a stand mixer fitted with a dough hook, combine all the ingredients. Gradually add 1½–1⅔ cups (12–14 oz/350–400 ml) of lukewarm water and mix on medium speed for 10 minutes, until the dough is soft and comes away from the sides of the bowl.

② Shape the dough into a ball, then place it in a lightly floured bowl. Cover with a cloth and set aside to rise for 1½ hours.

③ Punch down (deflate) the dough and shape it into a round loaf. Line a 9-inch (23-cm) Dutch oven (casserole) with parchment paper. Add the dough inside and proof (prove) for 1 hour.

④ Using a knife, score the top of the loaf with decorative cuts. If desired, dust flour over the surface of the dough to enhance its appearance and texture. Cover the pan and place it in a cold oven.

⑤ Preheat the oven to 475°F (240°C/Gas mark 9).

⑥ Bake the bread for 40 minutes. Transfer the loaf to a cooling rack and set aside to cool completely.

⑦ Slice, then serve.

YOGURT CAKE

(V) (NF)

PREPARATION TIME:
10 minutes

COOKING TIME:
1 hour

Makes: 1 cake

2 ½ cups (10 ½ oz/300 g) all-purpose (plain) flour	Scant 1 cup (7 fl oz/200 ml) milk
1 ½ cups (10 ½ oz/300 g) sugar	Scant 1 cup (7 fl oz/200 ml) sunflower oil
2 ¼ teaspoons baking powder	3 eggs
2 teaspoons vanilla sugar	2 teaspoons butter, room temperature
½ cup (4 fl oz/120 ml) plain yogurt	1 teaspoon vanilla extract

① Preheat the oven to 350°F (180°C/Gas mark 4). Grease an 8-inch (20-cm) Dutch oven.
② Combine all the ingredients in the pan and mix vigorously with a wooden spoon until the batter is smooth. Cover the casserole and bake for 50 minutes.
③ Remove the lid and bake for another 10 minutes.
④ Serve.

ONE-POT BRIOCHE

(V) (NF)

PREPARATION TIME:
25 minutes, plus 1½–2½ hours resting time

COOKING TIME:
40 minutes

Makes: 1 loaf

½ oz (12 g) cake (fresh) yeast

⅔ cup (5 fl oz/150 ml) lukewarm milk, plus extra for glazing

3 ⅓ cups (14 oz/400 g) all-purpose (plain) flour

½ cup (4 ¼ oz/120 g) butter, room temperature

2 egg yolks, plus 1 for glazing

⅓ cup (2 ¾ oz/80 g) sugar

1 teaspoon salt

Pearl sugar (optional)

① Dissolve the yeast in a little warm milk and set aside for 10 minutes.
② In a stand mixer fitted with a dough hook, combine the flour, the remaining lukewarm milk, butter, 2 egg yolks, sugar, and dissolved yeast. Mix on medium speed for 1 minute, then add the salt and knead until the dough is smooth and comes away from the sides of the bowl. (Alternatively, knead by hand.)
③ Shape the dough into a ball and place it in a bowl. Cover with a cloth and set aside in a warm environment for 1–2 hours, until doubled in size.
④ Punch down (deflate) the dough, then cut it into 8 equal portions. Shape them into balls and arrange them in a 9-inch (23-cm) Dutch oven (casserole). Proof for 30 minutes.
⑤ Mix the remaining egg yolk with a little milk and brush it over the top of the brioche. Sprinkle with pearl sugar, if using. Cover the pan, then place in a cold oven and heat to 350°F (180°C/Gas mark 4). Bake for 40 minutes.
⑥ Serve.

PEAR AND ALMOND CAKE

(v)

PREPARATION TIME:
10 minutes

COOKING TIME:
30 minutes

Makes: 1 cake

4 eggs

½ cup (3 ½ oz/100 g) sugar

½ cup (4 ¼ fl oz/120 g) plain yogurt

3 ½ tablespoons milk

⅔ cup (2 ¾ oz/80 g) all-purpose flour

1 cup (4 ¼ oz/120 g) almond meal

1 ¼ teaspoons baking powder

3 pears, peeled, cored, and thinly sliced

Sliced almonds, for sprinkling (optional)

① Preheat the oven to 350°F (180°C/Gas mark 4). Grease a 9-inch (23-cm) Dutch oven (casserole).

② Beat the eggs and sugar in a bowl until well combined. Add the yogurt and milk. Mix in the flour, almond meal, and baking powder until smooth.

③ Fold the pears into the batter. Pour the batter into the prepared pan. Sprinkle with sliced almonds, if using. Cover and bake for 30 minutes, until a knife inserted in the center comes out clean.

④ Slice, then serve.

STEWED PINEAPPLE WITH VANILLA

PREPARATION TIME:
10 minutes

COOKING TIME:
50 minutes

Serves: 4

1¼ cups (9 oz/250 g) cane sugar

1 pineapple, peeled, cored, and cut into chunks

2 vanilla beans

① Combine the sugar and 1¼ cups (10 fl oz/300 ml) of water in a Dutch oven (casserole). Place over low heat until the sugar has dissolved. Add the pineapple and stir well.
② Split the vanilla beans, scrape the seeds into the pan, and add the pods. Partially cover the pan and cook over low heat for 45 minutes.
③ Serve.

BAKED APPLES WITH COOKIE CRUMB

PREPARATION TIME:
10 minutes

COOKING TIME:
35 minutes

Serves: 4

4 Royal Gala apples

2 tablespoons honey

4 Belgian spice cookies (speculoos), coarsely crumbled

① Preheat the oven to 350°F (180°C/Gas mark 4). Slice off the tops of the apples to use as caps.
② Core the apples with an apple corer, then scoop out the flesh with a melon baller, being careful not to damage the skin. Chop the flesh and place it into a bowl.
③ Set aside a small portion of the cookie (biscuit) crumbs for topping. Add the remaining crumbs and honey to the bowl of apples, then mix well.
④ Fill the apples with the mixture, sprinkle with the reserved crumbled cookies, and replace their caps.
⑤ Place the apples in ovenproof mini Dutch ovens (casseroles) and bake for 30–35 minutes.
⑥ Serve warm.

RICE PUDDING

(V) (GF) (NF) (-5)

PREPARATION TIME:
5 minutes

COOKING TIME:
40 minutes

Serves: 6

¾ cup (6 oz/180 g) short-grain rice

4 ¼ cups (34 fl oz/1 liter) whole milk

⅓ cup (2 ¾ oz/80 g) sugar

1 vanilla bean

① Rinse the rice quickly under cold running water.
② Combine the milk and sugar in a Dutch oven (casserole). Split the vanilla bean, scrape the seeds into the pan, and add the pod. Bring to a boil.
③ Add the rice, then reduce the heat to low. Cook for 40 minutes, stirring regularly, until the pudding is creamy and slightly runny. (The rice will continue to absorb the excess milk as it cools.)
④ Remove the vanilla pod, then set the pudding aside to cool. Ladle into ramekins and refrigerate until set.
⑤ Serve warm.

MENUS

CLASSICS OF FRENCH CUISINE

Basque-Style Veal Stew 178
Beef Bourguignon 138
Beef with Carrots 144
Bouillabaisse 54
Chicken Pot Roast 94
Classic Cheese Fondue 30
Coq au Vin 80
Flemish Beef Stew 142
Lamb Navarin 194
Lentil Stew with Salt Pork and Sausages 126
Pistou Soup 14
Pot-au-Feu 140
Provençal Beef Stew 158
Quick and Easy Cassoulet 118
Rabbit in Mustard Sauce 104
Ratatouille 24
Rice Pudding 218
Sausages and Sauerkraut 112
Slow-Braised Leg of Lamb 196
Veal Blanquette 164
Veal Veal Marengo 176

EVERYDAY MEALS

Baked Apples with Cookie Crumb 216
Beef Noodle Soup 136
Beer-Braised Chicken 82
Creamy Beef with Potatoes 150
Cauliflower and Lentil Mujadara 16
Chicken Ramen 76
Coconut-Lime Mussels 60
Coconut-Mango Veal Curry 182
Curried Quinoa Broccoli Bowl 40
Curry Coconut Chicken Noodles 84
Eggplant and Rigatoni Casserole 34
Indian-Style Vegetable Curry 38
Lasagna Casserole 154
Lentil and Sweet Potato Dal 44
Mexican-Style Soup 114
Moroccan Lamb and Chickpea Chorba 186
Mushroom Risotto 18

Pear and Almond Cake 212
Pork Tenderloin in Cream Sauce 124
Pork Tenderloin with Orange-Honey Glaze 130
Quick and Easy Cassoulet 118
Quick and Easy Chili con Carne 146
Rice Pudding 218
Shrimp and Rice Skillet 66
Southwest Chicken Quinoa 93
Spiced Chicken and Lentils 72
Stuffed Zucchini and Tomatoes 120
Thai Shrimp Curry 64
Tortellini Stew 32
Turkey and Butternut Squash Stew 98
Veal and Mushroom Tagliatelle 168
Vegetable Soba Noodles 20

FLAVORS FROM AROUND THE WORLD

Beef Biryani 160
Beef Noodle Soup 136
Catalan-Style Seafood Stew 68
Cauliflower and Lentil Mujadara 16
Chicken Ramen 76
Chicken Tagine with Dried Apricots 86
Chicken Tagine with Preserved Lemons 88
Coconut Split Pea Curry 42
Coconut-Mango Veal Curry 182
Colombo-Spiced Pork and Sweet Potato Stew 132
Curried Quinoa Broccoli Bowl 40
Curry Coconut Chicken Noodles 84
Fasolada 26
Hungarian Goulash 152
Indian-Style Vegetable Curry 38
Lamb Kofta and Fava Bean Tagine 190
Lamb Tikka Masala 188
Lasagna Casserole 154
Lentil and Sweet Potato Dal 44
Mexican-Style Soup 114
Moroccan Lamb and Chickpea Chorba 186
Moroccan-Style Fish Stew 56
Osso Buco 162
Pulled Pork 116
Quick and Easy Chili con Carne 146
Sicilian Caponata 22
Spiced Chicken and Lentils 72
Thai Shrimp Curry 64
Vegetable Soba Noodles 20
Vegetable Tagine 28
West African–Style Beef Stew 141

INDEX

Page numbers in *italics* indicate photos.

5 ingredients or fewer
baked apples with cookie crumb 216, *217*
easy bread 206, *207*
easy monkfish casserole 52, *53*
garlic-sage pork roast 128, *129*
popcorn 204, *205*
rice pudding 218, *219*
stewed pineapple with vanilla 214, *215*

30 minutes or less
beef noodle soup 136, *137*
classic cheese fondue 30, *31*
coconut-lime mussels 60, *61*
curry coconut chicken noodles 84, *85*
popcorn 204, *205*
shrimp and rice skillet 66, *67*
Southwest chicken quinoa 93
vegetable soba noodles 20, *21*

A
alcohol
beer-braised chicken 82, *83*
calamari in tomato sauce 62, *63*
classic cheese fondue 30, *31*
see also **beer; cider, hard; wine**

ale
beer-braised beef stew 148, *149*
beer-braised veal roulades 174, *175*
Flemish beef stew 142, *143*

almond meal
pear and almond cake 212, *213*

almonds
Catalan-style seafood stew 68, *69*

American Munster cheese
creamy chicken skillet 78, *79*

apples
baked apples with cookie crumb 216, *217*
beer-braised veal roulades 174, *175*
creamy cider chicken with apples 74, *75*

apricots, dried
chicken tagine with dried apricots 86, *87*

aubergines *see* **eggplants**
axoa 178, *179*

B
bacon
beef Bourguignon 138, *139*
lentil stew with salt pork and sausages 126, *127*
Provençal beef stew 158, *159*
sausages and sauerkraut 112, *113*

baking
about 9
baked apples with cookie crumb 216, *217*
cod and chorizo bake 50, *51*

barbecue sauce
pulled pork 116, *117*

basil
pistou soup 14, *15*
Basque chicken 92
Basque-style veal stew 178, *179*

beans
lamb kofta and fava bean tagine 190, *191*
see also **green beans; kidney beans; navy beans; white beans**

béchamel sauce
spinach and ricotta cannelloni 36, *37*

beef
about 9
beef biryani 160, *161*
beef Bourguignon 138, *139*
beef hot pot 156, *157*
beef noodle soup 136, *137*
beef with carrots 144, *145*
beer-braised beef stew 148, *149*
creamy beef with potatoes 150, *151*
Flemish beef stew 142, *143*
Hungarian goulash 152, *153*
lasagna casserole 154, *155*
pot-au-feu 140
Provençal beef stew 158, *159*
quick and easy chili con carne 146, *147*
West African-style beef stew 141

beer
beer-braised beef stew 148, *149*
beer-braised chicken 82, *83*
beer-braised veal roulades 174, *175*
see also **ale; lager**

Belgian spice cookies *see* **cookies, Belgian spice**
Belgian-style fish stew 58, *59*

bell peppers
Basque chicken 92
Basque-style veal stew 178, *179*
beef biryani 160, *161*
coconut-mango veal curry 182, *183*
cod and chorizo bake 50, *51*
Hungarian goulash 152, *153*
Mexican-style soup 114, *115*
Moroccan lamb and chickpea chorba 186, *187*
Moroccan-style fish stew 56, *57*
quick and easy chili con carne 146, *147*
ratatouille 24, *25*
shrimp and rice skillet 66, *67*
Southwest chicken quinoa 93
tortellini stew 32, *33*

biryani
beef biryani 160, *161*
bouillabaisse 54, *55*
Boursin® *see* **cheese spread**

boy choy
beef noodle soup 136, *137*
chicken ramen 76, *77*

braising
about 9
braised veal with carrots and walnuts 172, *173*
cider-braised lamb shanks 198, *199*
slow-braised leg of lamb 196, *197*

bread (ingredient)
Catalan-style seafood stew 68, *69*
chicken pot roast 94, *95*
classic cheese fondue 30, *31*
see also **gingerbread**

bread (recipe)
easy bread 206, *207*

brioche
one-pot brioche 210, *211*

broad beans *see* **fava beans**

broccoli
curried quinoa broccoli bowl 40, *41*
browning 9

butternut squash
hearty chickpea stew 27
turkey and butternut squash stew 98, *99*

222   INDEX

C

cakes
    pear and almond cake 212, *213*
    yogurt cake 208, *209*

calamari
    calamari in tomato sauce 62, *63*
    Catalan-style seafood stew 68, *69*

cannelloni
    spinach and ricotta cannelloni 36, *37*

capers
    Sicilian caponata 22, *23*

caponata
    Sicilian caponata 22, *23*

caramelizing 9

carrots
    beef Bourguignon 138, *139*
    beef hot pot 156, *157*
    beef noodle soup 136, *137*
    beef with carrots 144, *145*
    beer-braised beef stew 148, *149*
    Belgian-style fish stew 58, *59*
    braised veal with carrots and walnuts 172, *173*
    chicken pot roast 94, *95*
    chicken ramen 76, *77*
    coconut split pea curry 42, *43*
    creamy veal and vegetable stew 170, *171*
    curry coconut chicken noodles 84, *85*
    duck à l'orange 102, *103*
    fasolada 26
    hearty chickpea stew 27
    lamb navarin 194, *195*
    lamb tikka masala 188, *189*
    lentil and sausage soup 110, *111*
    lentil stew with salt pork and sausages 126, *127*
    Mexican-style soup 114, *115*
    Moroccan-style fish stew 56, *57*
    one-pot salmon 48, *49*
    pistou soup 14, *15*
    pot-au-feu 140
    Provençal beef stew 158, *159*
    quick and easy cassoulet 118, *119*
    veal and chorizo bean stew 166, *167*
    veal blanquette 164, *165*
    veal Marengo 176, *177*
    vegetable soba noodles 20, *21*
    vegetable tagine 28, *29*

casserole (pot) *see* Dutch oven

casseroles
    easy monkfish casserole 52, *53*
    eggplant and rigatoni casserole 34, *35*
    lasagna casserole 154, *155*

cassoulets
    quick and easy cassoulet 118, *119*
    Catalan-style seafood stew 68, *69*

cauliflower
    cauliflower and lentil mujadara 16, *17*
    hearty chickpea stew 27

celery
    beef hot pot 156, *157*
    Belgian-style fish stew 58, *59*
    bouillabaisse 54, *55*
    chicken pot roast 94, *95*
    lentil and sausage soup 110, *111*
    Mexican-style soup 114, *115*
    Moroccan-style fish stew 56, *57*
    one-pot salmon 48, *49*
    osso buco 162, *163*
    pot-au-feu 140

cheese
    classic cheese fondue 30, *31*
    creamy chicken skillet 78, *79*
    lasagna casserole 154, *155*
    see also **mozzarella; Parmesan; ricotta cheese**

cheese spread
    guinea fowl with chestnuts and peas 106, *107*
    shrimp and rice skillet 66, *67*
    turkey roulade with mushrooms 100, *101*
    veal and mushroom tagliatelle 168, *169*

chestnuts
    guinea fowl with chestnuts and peas 106, *107*
    turkey and butternut squash stew 98, *99*

chicken
    Basque chicken 92
    beer-braised chicken 82, *83*
    chicken fricassee 90, *91*
    chicken pot roast 94, *95*
    chicken ramen 76, *77*
    chicken tagine with dried apricots 86, *87*
    chicken tagine with preserved lemons 88, *89*
    coq au vin 80, *81*
    creamy chicken skillet 78, *79*
    creamy cider chicken with apples 74, *75*
    curry coconut chicken noodles 84, *85*
    farmhouse chicken with samphire 96, *97*
    Southwest chicken quinoa 93
    spiced chicken and lentils 72, *73*

chickpeas
    curried quinoa broccoli bowl 40, *41*
    hearty chickpea stew 27
    Mexican-style soup 114, *115*
    Moroccan lamb and chickpea chorba 186, *187*
    Moroccan-style fish stew 56, *57*
    one-pot salmon 48, *49*

chili
    quick and easy chili con carne 146, *147*

chorba
    Moroccan lamb and chickpea chorba 186, *187*

chorizo
    cod and chorizo bake 50, *51*
    Mexican-style soup 114, *115*
    veal and chorizo bean stew 166, *167*

choy sum
    chicken ramen 76, *77*

cider, hard
    cider-braised lamb shanks 198, *199*
    creamy cider chicken with apples 74, *75*

cilantro (coriander)
    beef biryani 160, *161*
    Indian-style vegetable curry 38, *39*
    spiced chicken and lentils 72, *73*
    vegetable soba noodles 20, *21*
    vegetable tagine 28, *29*

clams
    Catalan-style seafood stew 68, *69*

classic cheese fondue 30, *31*

coconut milk
    coconut-lime mussels 60, *61*
    coconut split pea curry 42, *43*
    coconut-mango veal curry 182, *183*
    curried quinoa broccoli bowl 40, *41*
    curry coconut chicken noodles 84, *85*
    lamb tikka masala 188, *189*
    spiced chicken and lentils 72, *73*
    Thai shrimp curry 64, *65*

cod
    Belgian-style fish stew 58, *59*
    Catalan-style seafood stew 68, *69*
    cod and chorizo bake 50, *51*
    Moroccan-style fish stew 56, *57*

cognac
    calamari in tomato sauce 62, *63*
    Colombo-spiced pork and sweet potato stew 132, *133*

Comté cheese
    classic cheese fondue 30, *31*

cookies, Belgian spice
    baked apples with cookie crumb 216, *217*
    beer-braised veal roulades 174, *175*
    coq au vin 80, *81*

coriander *see* **cilantro**

corn
    Mexican-style soup 114, *115*
    Southwest chicken quinoa 93

Cornish game hens
    guinea fowl with chestnuts and peas 106, *107*

courgettes *see* **zucchinis**

couscous
    vegetable tagine 28, *29*

cream, light
    creamy chicken skillet 78, *79*
    creamy veal and vegetable stew 170, *171*
    see also **whipping cream**

creamy beef with potatoes 150, *151*

creamy chicken skillet 78, *79*
creamy cider chicken with apples 74, *75*
creamy veal and vegetable stew 170, *171*
crème fraîche
   Belgian-style fish stew 58, *59*
   braised veal with carrots and walnuts 172, *173*
   chicken fricassee 90, *91*
   coq au vin 80, *81*
   creamy beef with potatoes 150, *151*
   creamy cider chicken with apples 74, *75*
   farmhouse chicken with samphire 96, *97*
   rabbit in mustard sauce 104, *105*
   turkey roulades with mushrooms 100, *101*
   veal blanquette 164, *165*
curries
   coconut split pea curry 42, *43*
   coconut-mango veal curry 182, *183*
   curried quinoa broccoli bowl 40, *41*
   curry coconut chicken noodles 84, *85*
   Indian-style vegetable curry 38, *39*
   Thai shrimp curry 64, *65*

D
dairy-free recipes
   baked apples with cookie crumb 216, *217*
   Basque chicken 92
   Basque-style veal stew 178, *179*
   beef Bourguignon 138, *139*
   beef hot pot 156, *157*
   beef noodle soup 136, *137*
   beef with carrots 144, *145*
   beer-braised beef stew 148, *149*
   bouillabaisse 54, *55*
   calamari in tomato sauce 62, *63*
   Catalan-style seafood stew 68, *69*
   cauliflower and lentil mujadara 16, *17*

chicken pot roast 94, *95*
chicken ramen 76, *77*
chicken tagine with dried apricots 86, *87*
chicken tagine with preserved lemons 88, *89*
cider-braised lamb shanks 198, *199*
coconut-lime mussels 60, *61*
coconut split pea curry 42, *43*
coconut-mango veal curry 182, *183*
cod and chorizo bake 50, *51*
Colombo-spiced pork and sweet potato stew 132, *133*
curried quinoa broccoli bowl 40, *41*
curry coconut chicken noodles 84, *85*
duck à l'orange 102, *103*
easy bread 206, *207*
easy monkfish casserole 52, *53*
fasolada 26
hearty chickpea stew 27
herbed lamb with potatoes and peas 192, *193*
Hungarian goulash 152, *153*
Indian-style vegetable curry 38, *39*
lamb kofta and fava bean tagine 190, *191*
lamb shanks with garlic and thyme 200, *201*
lentil and sausage soup 110, *111*
lentil and sweet potato dal 44, *45*
lentil stew with salt pork and sausages 126, *127*
Mexican-style soup 114, *115*
Moroccan lamb and chickpea chorba 186, *187*
Moroccan-style fish stew 56, *57*
one-pot salmon 48, *49*
osso buco 162, *163*
popcorn 204, *205*
pork tenderloin with orange-honey glaze 130, *131*
pot-au-feu 140
Provençal beef stew 158, *159*

pulled pork 116, *117*
quick and easy cassoulet 118, *119*
quick and easy chili con carne 146, *147*
ratatouille 24, *25*
sausages and sauerkraut 112, *113*
Sicilian caponata 22, *23*
Southwest chicken quinoa 93
spiced chicken and lentils 72, *73*
stewed pineapple with vanilla 214, *215*
stuffed zucchini and tomatoes 120, *121*
Thai shrimp curry 64, *65*
tortellini stew 32, *33*
veal and chorizo bean stew 166, *167*
veal Marengo 176, *177*
vegetable soba noodles 20, *21*
vegetable tagine 28, *29*
West African-style beef stew 141
dal
   lentil and sweet potato dal 44, *45*
desserts *see* sweets
duck
   duck à l'orange 102, *103*
   quick and easy cassoulet 118, *119*
Dutch gin (jenever)
   beer-braised chicken 82, *83*
Dutch oven (casserole) about 9

E
easy bread 206, *207*
easy monkfish casserole 52, *53*
eggplants (aubergines)
   Colombo-spiced pork and sweet potato stew 132, *133*
   eggplant and rigatoni casserole 34, *35*
   Indian-style vegetable curry 38, *39*
   ratatouille 24, *25*
   Sicilian caponata 22, *23*
   tortellini stew 32, *33*
eggs
   Belgian-style fish stew 58, *59*

chicken pot roast 94, *95*
chicken ramen 76, *77*
creamy beef with potatoes 150, *151*
lentil and sweet potato dal 44, *45*
one-pot brioche 210, *211*
pear and almond cake 212, *213*
turkey and butternut squash stew 98, *99*
veal blanquette 164, *165*
yogurt cake 208, *209*
Emmental cheese
   classic cheese fondue 30, *31*

F
farmhouse chicken with samphire 96, *97*
fasolada 26
fava (broad) beans
   lamb kofta and fava bean tagine 190, *191*
fennel
   bouillabaisse 54, *55*
   vegetable tagine 28, *29*
fish
   Belgian-style fish stew 58, *59*
   bouillabaisse 54, *55*
   easy monkfish casserole 52, *53*
   Moroccan-style fish stew 56, *57*
   one-pot salmon 48, *49*
   see also **cod**
Flemish beef stew 142, *143*
Flemish veal stew 180, *181*
fondue
   classic cheese fondue 30, *31*

G
game
   guinea fowl with chestnuts and peas 106, *107*
   rabbit in mustard sauce 104, *105*
garlic
   garlic-sage pork roast 128, *129*
   lamb shanks with garlic and thyme 200, *201*
gingerbread
   chicken tagine with dried apricots 86, *87*
   Flemish beef stew 142, *143*
gluten-free recipes
   Basque chicken 92

Basque-style veal stew 178, *179*
beef biryani 160, *161*
Belgian-style fish stew 58, *59*
bouillabaisse 54, *55*
braised veal with carrots and walnuts 172, *173*
calamari in tomato sauce 62, *63*
cauliflower and lentil mujadara 16, *17*
chicken fricassee 90, *91*
chicken tagine with preserved lemons 88, *89*
cider-braised lamb shanks 198, *199*
coconut-lime mussels 60, *61*
coconut split pea curry 42, *43*
coconut-mango veal curry 182, *183*
cod and chorizo bake 50, *51*
Colombo-spiced pork and sweet potato stew 132, *133*
creamy beef with potatoes 150, *151*
creamy veal and vegetable stew 170, *171*
curried quinoa broccoli bowl 40, *41*
curry coconut chicken noodles 84, *85*
duck à l'orange 102, *103*
easy monkfish casserole 52, *53*
fasolada 26
garlic-sage pork roast 128, *129*
guinea fowl with chestnuts and peas 106, *107*
hearty chickpea stew 27
herbed lamb with potatoes and peas 192, *193*
Hungarian goulash 152, *153*
Indian-style vegetable curry 38, *39*
lamb kofta and fava bean tagine 190, *191*
lamb shanks with garlic and thyme 200, *201*
lamb tikka masala 188, *189*
lentil and sausage soup 110, *111*
lentil and sweet potato dal 44, *45*

lentil stew with salt pork and sausages 126, *127*
Mexican-style soup 114, *115*
Moroccan-style fish stew 56, *57*
mushroom risotto 18, *19*
one-pot salmon 48, *49*
popcorn 204, *205*
porchetta with minted peas 122, *123*
pork tenderloin in cream sauce 124, *125*
pork tenderloin with orange-honey glaze 130, *131*
pot-au-feu 140
quick and easy cassoulet 118, *119*
quick and easy chili con carne 146, *147*
rabbit in mustard sauce 104, *105*
ratatouille 24, *25*
rice pudding 218, *219*
sausages and sauerkraut 112, *113*
shrimp and rice skillet 66, *67*
Sicilian caponata 22, *23*
slow-braised leg of lamb 196, *197*
Southwest chicken quinoa 93
spiced chicken and lentils 72, *73*
stewed pineapple with vanilla 214, *215*
stuffed zucchini and tomatoes 120, *121*
turkey and butternut squash stew 98, *99*
veal and chorizo bean stew 166, *167*
veal Marengo 176, *177*
West African-style beef stew 141
goulash
 Hungarian goulash 152, *153*
green beans
 lamb navarin 194, *195*
 pistou soup 14, *15*
green onions *see* **scallions**
guinea fowl
 guinea fowl with chestnuts and peas 106, *107*

H
ham
 Basque chicken 92
 Basque-style veal stew 178, *179*
 chicken pot roast 94, *95*
 easy monkfish casserole 52, *53*
 hearty chickpea stew 27
hens
 chicken pot roast 94, *95*
 guinea fowl with chestnuts and peas 106, *107*
 herbed lamb with potatoes and peas 192, *193*
honey
 pork tenderloin with orange-honey glaze 130, *131*
hot pot
 beef hot pot 156, *157*
Hungarian goulash 152, *153*

I
Indian-style vegetable curry 38, *39*

J
jenever *see* **Dutch gin**
juniper berries
 beef hot pot 156, *157*
 sausages and sauerkraut 112, *113*

K
kale
 chicken pot roast 94, *95*
kidney beans
 Mexican-style soup 114, *115*
 pistou soup 14, *15*
 quick and easy chili con carne 146, *147*
 Southwest chicken quinoa 93
kirsch
 classic cheese fondue 30, *31*
koftas
 lamb kofta and fava bean tagine 190, *191*

L
lager
 beer-braised chicken 82, *83*
 creamy chicken skillet 78, *79*
 Flemish veal stew 180, *181*
lamb
 about 9

 beef hot pot 156, *157*
 cider-braised lamb shanks 198, *199*
 herbed lamb with potatoes and peas 192, *193*
 lamb kofta and fava bean tagine 190, *191*
 lamb navarin 194, *195*
 lamb shanks with garlic and thyme 200, *201*
 lamb tikka masala 188, *189*
 Moroccan lamb and chickpea chorba 186, *187*
 slow-braised leg of lamb 196, *197*
lardons
 beer-braised chicken 82, *83*
 guinea fowl with chestnuts and peas 106, *107*
 quick and easy cassoulet 118, *119*
lasagna
 lasagna casserole 154, *155*
leeks
 beef hot pot 156, *157*
 Belgian-style fish stew 58, *59*
 bouillabaisse 54, *55*
 chicken pot roast 94, *95*
 Mexican-style soup 114, *115*
 pistou soup 14, *15*
 pot-au-feu 140
 veal blanquette 164, *165*
lemon juice
 beer-braised chicken 82, *83*
lemongrass
 curry coconut chicken noodles 84, *85*
 Thai shrimp curry 64, *65*
lemons
 chicken tagine with preserved lemons 88, *89*
 slow-braised leg of lamb 196, *197*
lentils
 cauliflower and lentil mujadara 16, *17*
 lentil and sausage soup 110, *111*
 lentil and sweet potato dal 44, *45*
 lentil stew with salt pork and sausages 126, *127*
 spiced chicken and lentils 72, *73*
Limburger cheese
 creamy chicken skillet 78, *79*

lime juice, leaves, or zest
  coconut-lime mussels 60, *61*
  Colombo-spiced pork and sweet potato stew 132, *133*
  curry coconut chicken noodles 84, *85*
  Thai shrimp curry 64, *65*

M

mafé 141
mango
  coconut-mango veal curry 182, *183*
marinating 9
Maroilles cheese
  creamy chicken skillet 78, *79*
marrow bones
  pot-au-feu 140
mascarpone cheese
  lasagna casserole 154, *155*
meat
  about 9
  see also specific meats
menus 220–3
Mexican-style soup 114, *115*
milk
  garlic-sage pork roast 128, *129*
  one-pot brioche 210, *211*
  pear and almond cake 212, *213*
  rice pudding 218, *219*
  spinach and ricotta cannelloni 36, *37*
  yogurt cake 208, *209*
mint
  beef biryani 160, *161*
  porchetta with minted peas 122, *123*
monkfish
  easy monkfish casserole 52, *53*
  Moroccan lamb and chickpea chorba 186, *187*
Moroccan-style fish stew 56, *57*
mozzarella
  eggplant and rigatoni casserole 34, *35*
  lasagna casserole 154, *155*
mujadara
  cauliflower and lentil mujadara 16, *17*
mushrooms
  beef Bourguignon 138, *139*
  beer-braised chicken 82, *83*
  braised veal with carrots and walnuts 172, *173*
  chicken fricassee 90, *91*
  chicken ramen 76, *77*
  coq au vin 80, *81*
  creamy veal and vegetable stew 170, *171*
  Flemish veal stew 180, *181*
  lentil and sweet potato dal 44, *45*
  mushroom risotto 18, *19*
  pork tenderloin in cream sauce 124, *125*
  shrimp and rice skillet 66, *67*
  turkey roulade with mushrooms 100, *101*
  veal and mushroom tagliatelle 168, *169*
  veal blanquette 164, *165*
  veal Marengo 176, *177*
  vegetable soba noodles 20, *21*
mussels
  Catalan-style seafood stew 68, *69*
  coconut-lime mussels 60, *61*
mustard
  rabbit in mustard sauce 104, *105*

N

navarin
  lamb navarin 194, *195*
navy beans
  fasolada 26
  pistou soup 14, *15*
noodles
  beef noodle soup 136, *137*
  chicken ramen 76, *77*
  curry coconut chicken noodles 84, *85*
  vegetable soba noodles 20, *21*
nut-free recipes
  baked apples with cookie crumb 216, *217*
  Basque chicken 92
  Basque-style veal stew 178, *179*
  beef biryani 160, *161*
  beef Bourguignon 138, *139*
  beef hot pot 156, *157*
  beef noodle soup 136, *137*
  beef with carrots 144, *145*
  beer-braised beef stew 148, *149*
  beer-braised chicken 82, *83*
  beer-braised veal roulades 174, *175*
  Belgian-style fish stew 58, *59*
  bouillabaisse 54, *55*
  calamari in tomato sauce 62, *63*
  chicken fricassee 90, *91*
  chicken pot roast 94, *95*
  chicken ramen 76, *77*
  chicken tagine with dried apricots 86, *87*
  chicken tagine with preserved lemons 88, *89*
  cider-braised lamb shanks 198, *199*
  classic cheese fondue 30, *31*
  coconut-lime mussels 60, *61*
  coconut split pea curry 42, *43*
  coconut-mango veal curry 182, *183*
  cod and chorizo bake 50, *51*
  Colombo-spiced pork and sweet potato stew 132, *133*
  coq au vin 80, *81*
  creamy beef with potatoes 150, *151*
  creamy chicken skillet 78, *79*
  creamy cider chicken with apples 74, *75*
  creamy veal and vegetable stew 170, *171*
  curried quinoa broccoli bowl 40, *41*
  curry coconut chicken noodles 84, *85*
  duck à l'orange 102, *103*
  easy bread 206, *207*
  easy monkfish casserole 52, *53*
  eggplant and rigatoni casserole 34, *35*
  farmhouse chicken with samphire 96, *97*
  fasolada 26
  Flemish beef stew 142, *143*
  Flemish veal stew 180, *181*
  garlic-sage pork roast 128, *129*
  hearty chickpea stew 27
  herbed lamb with potatoes and peas 192, *193*
  Hungarian goulash 152, *153*
  Indian-style vegetable curry 38, *39*
  lamb kofta and fava bean tagine 190, *191*
  lamb navarin 194, *195*
  lamb shanks with garlic and thyme 200, *201*
  lamb tikka masala 188, *189*
  lasagna casserole 154, *155*
  lentil and sausage soup 110, *111*
  lentil and sweet potato dal 44, *45*
  lentil stew with salt pork and sausages 126, *127*
  Mexican-style soup 114, *115*
  Moroccan lamb and chickpea chorba 186, *187*
  Moroccan-style fish stew 56, *57*
  mushroom risotto 18, *19*
  One-Pot Salmon 48, *49*
  one-pot brioche 210, *211*
  osso buco 162, *163*
  pistou soup 14, *15*
  popcorn 204, *205*
  porchetta with minted peas 122, *123*
  pork tenderloin in cream sauce 124, *125*
  pork tenderloin with orange-honey glaze 130, *131*
  pot-au-feu 140
  Provençal beef stew 158, *159*
  pulled pork 116, *117*
  quick and easy cassoulet 118, *119*
  quick and easy chili con carne 146, *147*
  rabbit in mustard sauce 104, *105*
  ratatouille 24, *25*
  rice pudding 218, *219*
  sausages and sauerkraut 112, *113*
  shrimp and rice skillet 66, *67*
  Sicilian caponata 22, *23*
  slow-braised leg of lamb 196, *197*
  Southwest chicken quinoa 93
  spiced chicken and lentils 72, *73*
  spinach and ricotta cannelloni 36, *37*
  stewed pineapple with vanilla 214, *215*

stuffed zucchini and tomatoes 120, *121*
Thai shrimp curry 64, *65*
tortellini stew 32, *33*
turkey roulade with mushrooms 100, *101*
veal and chorizo bean stew 166, *167*
veal and mushroom tagliatelle 168, *169*
veal blanquette 164, *165*
veal Marengo 176, *177*
vegetable soba noodles 20, *21*
vegetable tagine 28, *29*
yogurt cake 208, *209*

nuts
braised veal with carrots and walnuts 172, *173*
Catalan-style seafood stew 68, *69*
pear and almond cake 212, *213*
West African-style beef stew 141
see also **chestnuts**

O
olives
cod and chorizo bake 50, *51*
one-pot brioche 210, *211*
one-pot meals, about 7
one-pot salmon 48, *49*
onions
Basque chicken 92
Basque-style veal stew 178, *179*
beef biryani 160, *161*
beef Bourguignon 138, *139*
beef hot pot 156, *157*
beef noodle soup 136, *137*
beef with carrots 144, *145*
beer-braised beef stew 148, *149*
bouillabaisse 54, *55*
braised veal with carrots and walnuts 172, *173*
calamari in tomato sauce 62, *63*
Catalan-style seafood stew 68, *69*
cauliflower and lentil mujadara 16, *17*
chicken pot roast 94, *95*
chicken tagine with preserved lemons 88, *89*
cider-braised lamb shanks 198, *199*
coconut split pea curry 42, *43*
coconut-mango veal curry 182, *183*
Colombo-spiced pork and sweet potato stew 132, *133*
creamy beef with potatoes 150, *151*
creamy chicken skillet 78, *79*
curried quinoa broccoli bowl 40, *41*
curry coconut chicken noodles 84, *85*
eggplant and rigatoni casserole 34, *35*
fasolada 26
Flemish beef stew 142, *143*
Flemish veal stew 180, *181*
hearty chickpea stew 27
herbed lamb with potatoes and peas 192, *193*
Hungarian goulash 152, *153*
Indian-style vegetable curry 38, *39*
lamb shanks with garlic and thyme 200, *201*
lamb tikka masala 188, *189*
lasagna casserole 154, *155*
lentil and sausage soup 110, *111*
lentil and sweet potato dal 44, *45*
lentil stew with salt pork and sausages 126, *127*
Moroccan lamb and chickpea chorba 186, *187*
Moroccan-style fish stew 56, *57*
mushroom risotto 18, *19*
one-pot salmon 48, *49*
osso buco 162, *163*
pistou soup 14, *15*
porchetta with minted peas 122, *123*
pork tenderloin with orange-honey glaze 130, *131*
pot-au-feu 140
Provençal beef stew 158, *159*
quick and easy cassoulet 118, *119*
quick and easy chili con carne 146, *147*
ratatouille 24, *25*
sausages and sauerkraut 112, *113*
shrimp and rice skillet 66, *67*
Sicilian caponata 22, *23*
slow-braised leg of lamb 196, *197*
Southwest chicken quinoa 93
spiced chicken and lentils 72, *73*
stuffed zucchini and tomatoes 120, *121*
tortellini stew 32, *33*
turkey and butternut squash stew 98, *99*
turkey roulade with mushrooms 100, *101*
veal and chorizo bean stew 166, *167*
veal and mushroom tagliatelle 168, *169*
veal blanquette 164, *165*
vegetable soba noodles 20, *21*
vegetable tagine 28, *29*
West African-style beef stew 141
see also **pearl onions; red onions; scallions**
oranges
duck à l'orange 102, *103*
pork tenderloin with orange-honey glaze 130, *131*
osso buco 162, *163*

P
Parmesan
eggplant and rigatoni casserole 34, *35*
lasagna casserole 154, *155*
pistou soup 14, *15*
spinach and ricotta cannelloni 36, *37*
parsley
calamari in tomato sauce 62, *63*
Catalan-style seafood stew 68, *69*
chicken pot roast 94, *95*
lentil and sausage soup 110, *111*
pistou soup 14, *15*
rabbit in mustard sauce 104, *105*
shrimp and rice skillet 66, *67*
stuffed zucchini and tomatoes 120, *121*
parsnips
beer-braised beef stew 148, *149*
pot-au-feu 140
vegetable tagine 28, *29*
passata *see* **tomatoes, puréed**
pasta
eggplant and rigatoni casserole 34, *35*
lasagna casserole 154, *155*
Moroccan lamb and chickpea chorba 186, *187*
spinach and ricotta cannelloni 36, *37*
tortellini stew 32, *33*
turkey roulade with mushrooms 100, *101*
veal and mushroom tagliatelle 168, *169*
see also **noodles**
peanut butter
West African-style beef stew 141
pearl onions
beer-braised chicken 82, *83*
chicken fricassee 90, *91*
pears
pear and almond cake 212, *213*
peas
beef biryani 160, *161*
coconut split pea curry 42, *43*
curry coconut chicken noodles 84, *85*
guinea fowl with chestnuts and peas 106, *107*
herbed lamb with potatoes and peas 192, *193*
lamb navarin 194, *195*
lamb tikka masala 188, *189*
porchetta with minted peas 122, *123*
vegetable soba noodles 20, *21*
peppers, sweet
Basque-style veal stew 178, *179*
see also **bell peppers**
pesto
pistou soup 14, *15*
picada
Catalan-style seafood stew 68, *69*

pineapple
  stewed pineapple with vanilla 214, *215*
pistou soup 14, *15*
pollock
  Belgian-style fish stew 58, *59*
popcorn 204, *205*
porchetta with minted peas 122, *123*
pork
  about 9
  beef hot pot 156, *157*
  chicken pot roast 94, *95*
  Colombo-spiced pork and sweet potato stew 132, *133*
  easy monkfish casserole 52, *53*
  garlic-sage pork roast 128, *129*
  lentil stew with salt pork and sausages 126, *127*
  porchetta with minted peas 122, *123*
  pork tenderloin in cream sauce 124, *125*
  pork tenderloin with orange-honey glaze 130, *131*
  pulled pork 116, *117*
  stuffed zucchini and tomatoes 120, *121*
  see also **bacon; ham; sausages**
pot roasts
  chicken pot roast 94, *95*
potatoes
  beef hot pot 156, *157*
  beer-braised beef stew 148, *149*
  bouillabaisse 54, *55*
  creamy beef with potatoes 150, *151*
  creamy veal and vegetable stew 170, *171*
  easy monkfish casserole 52, *53*
  hearty chickpea stew 27
  herbed lamb with potatoes and peas 192, *193*
  Hungarian goulash 152, *153*
  pistou soup 14, *15*
  sausages and sauerkraut 112, *113*
  vegetable tagine 28, *29*
  see also **sweet potatoes**

pot-au-feu 140
poultry *see* **chicken; duck; turkey**
prosciutto
  chicken pot roast 94, *95*
  Provençal beef stew 158, *159*
puddings
  rice pudding 218, *219*
pulled pork 116, *117*
pumpkin
  beer-braised beef stew 148, *149*

Q
quick and easy cassoulet 118, *119*
quick and easy chili con carne 146, *147*
quinoa
  curried quinoa broccoli bowl 40, *41*
  Southwest chicken quinoa 93

R
rabbit
  rabbit in mustard sauce 104, *105*
ramen noodles
  chicken ramen 76, *77*
ratatouille 24, *25*
red kuri
  beer-braised beef stew 148, *149*
red onions
  chicken tagine with dried apricots 86, *87*
  lamb kofta and fava bean tagine 190, *191*
  Mexican-style soup 114, *115*
  pulled pork 116, *117*
rice
  beef biryani 160, *161*
  cauliflower and lentil mujadara 16, *17*
  mushroom risotto 18, *19*
  rice pudding 218, *219*
  shrimp and rice skillet 66, *67*
  stuffed zucchini and tomatoes 120, *121*
  turkey roulade with mushrooms 100, *101*
ricotta cheese
  lasagna casserole 154, *155*
  spinach and ricotta cannelloni 36, *37*

rigatoni
  eggplant and rigatoni casserole 34, *35*
risotto
  mushroom risotto 18, *19*
roasting
  about 9
  chicken pot roast 94, *95*
  garlic-sage pork roast 128, *129*
rutabaga (swede)
  chicken pot roast 94, *95*

S
sage
  garlic-sage pork roast 128, *129*
salmon
  one-pot salmon 48, *49*
samphire
  farmhouse chicken with samphire 96, *97*
sauerkraut
  sausages and sauerkraut 112, *113*
sausages
  lentil and sausage soup 110, *111*
  lentil stew with salt pork and sausages 126, *127*
  quick and easy cassoulet 118, *119*
  sausages and sauerkraut 112, *113*
  see also **chorizo**
scallions (green onions)
  chicken ramen 76, *77*
  curry coconut chicken noodles 84, *85*
  lamb navarin 194, *195*
seafood *see* **calamari; mussels; shrimp**
shallots
  beer-braised chicken 82, *83*
  beer-braised veal roulades 174, *175*
  braised veal with carrots and walnuts 172, *173*
  coconut-lime mussels 60, *61*
  cod and chorizo bake 50, *51*
  creamy veal and vegetable stew 170, *171*
  guinea fowl with chestnuts and peas 106, *107*
  pork tenderloin in cream sauce 124, *125*
  Thai shrimp curry 64, *65*

veal Marengo 176, *177*
shrimp
  Belgian-style fish stew 58, *59*
  Catalan-style seafood stew 68, *69*
  shrimp and rice skillet 66, *67*
  Thai shrimp curry 64, *65*
Sicilian caponata 22, *23*
slow cooking
  about 9
  slow-braised leg of lamb 196, *197*
snacks
  easy bread 206, *207*
  popcorn 204, *205*
soba noodles
  vegetable soba noodles 20, *21*
soups
  beef noodle soup 136, *137*
  chicken ramen 76, *77*
  fasolada 26
  lentil and sausage soup 110, *111*
  Mexican-style soup 114, *115*
  Moroccan lamb and chickpea chorba 186, *187*
  pistou soup 14, *15*
  Southwest chicken quinoa 93
soy sauce
  beef noodle soup 136, *137*
  chicken ramen 76, *77*
  vegetable soba noodles 20, *21*
speculoos *see* **cookies, Belgian spice**
spiced chicken and lentils 72, *73*
spinach
  spinach and ricotta cannelloni 36, *37*
split peas
  coconut split pea curry 42, *43*
spring onions *see* **scallions**
squash
  beer-braised beef stew 148, *149*
  see also **butternut squash**
squid *see* **calamari**
stewing
  about 9
  Basque-style veal stew 178, *179*
  beer-braised beef stew 148, *149*
  Belgian-style fish stew 58, *59*

Catalan-style seafood stew 68, 69
Colombo-spiced pork and sweet potato stew 132, 133
creamy veal and vegetable stew 170, 171
Flemish beef stew 142, 143
Flemish veal stew 180, 181
hearty chickpea stew 27
lentil stew with salt pork and sausages 126, 127
Moroccan-style fish stew 56, 57
Provençal beef stew 158, 159
stewed pineapple with vanilla 214, 215
tortellini stew 32, 33
turkey and butternut squash stew 98, 99
veal and chorizo bean stew 166, 167
West African-style beef stew 141
stuffed zuchini and tomatoes 120, 121
stuffing
chicken pot roast 94, 95
swede *see* **rutabaga**
sweet peppers
Basque-style veal stew 178, 179
sweet potatoes
Colombo-spiced pork and sweet potato stew 132, 133
Indian-style vegetable curry 38, 39
lentil and sweet potato dal 44, 45
West African-style beef stew 141
sweets
baked apples with cookie crumb 216, 217
one-pot brioche 210, 211
pear and almond cake 212, 213
rice pudding 218, 219
stewed pineapple with vanilla 214, 215
yogurt cake 208, 209

T
tagine
chicken tagine with dried apricots 86, 87
chicken tagine with preserved lemons 88, 89
lamb kofta and fava bean tagine 190, 191
vegetable tagine 28, 29
tagliatelle
veal and mushroom tagliatelle 168, 169
Thai shrimp curry 64, 65
thyme, fresh
lamb shanks with garlic and thyme 200, 201
tikka masala
lamb tikka masala 188, 189
tomatoes, canned
Basque chicken 92
calamari in tomato sauce 62, 63
Catalan-style seafood stew 68, 69
Colombo-spiced pork and sweet potato stew 132, 133
hearty chickpea stew 27
lamb navarin 194, 195
lamb tikka masala 188, 189
Mexican-style soup 114, 115
one-pot salmon 48, 49
quick and easy chili con carne 146, 147
veal Marengo 176, 177
tomatoes, fresh
bouillabaisse 54, 55
Catalan-style seafood stew 68, 69
cod and chorizo bake 50, 51
eggplant and rigatoni casserole 34, 35
fasolada 26
lamb kofta and fava bean tagine 190, 191
lentil and sweet potato dal 44, 45
Moroccan lamb and chickpea chorba 186, 187
Moroccan-style fish stew 56, 57
osso buco 162, 163
pistou soup 14, 15
ratatouille 24, 25
Sicilian caponata 22, 23
Southwest chicken quinoa 93
stuffed zucchini and tomatoes 120, 121

tortellini stew 32, 33
tomatoes, puréed (passata)
lasagna casserole 154, 155
tortellini
tortellini stew 32, 33
turkey
turkey and butternut squash stew 98, 99
turkey roulade with mushrooms 100, 101
turnips
Belgian-style fish stew 58, 59
chicken pot roast 94, 95
creamy veal and vegetable stew 170, 171
lamb navarin 194, 195
Moroccan-style fish stew 56, 57
pot-au-feu 140

V
vanilla beans
rice pudding 218, 219
stewed pineapple with vanilla 214, 215
veal
about 9
Basque-style veal stew 178, 179
beer-braised veal roulades 174, 175
braised veal with carrots and walnuts 172, 173
coconut-mango veal curry 182, 183
creamy veal and vegetable stew 170, 171
Flemish veal stew 180, 181
osso buco 162, 163
stuffed zucchini and tomatoes 120, 121
veal and chorizo bean stew 166, 167
veal and mushroom tagliatelle 168, 169
veal blanquette 164, 165
veal Marengo 176, 177
vegan recipes
cauliflower and lentil mujadara 16, 17
coconut split pea curry 42, 43
curried quinoa broccoli bowl 40, 41
easy bread 206, 207
fasolada 26

hearty chickpea stew 27
Indian-style vegetable curry 38, 39
popcorn 204, 205
ratatouille 24, 25
Sicilian caponata 22, 23
stewed pineapple with vanilla 214, 215
tortellini stew 32, 33
vegetable soba noodles 20, 21
vegetable tagine 28, 29
vegetables
Indian-style vegetable curry 38, 39
vegetable soba noodles 20, 21
vegetable tagine 28, 29
see also specific vegetables
vegetarian recipes
baked apples with cookie crumb 216, 217
cauliflower and lentil mujadara 16, 17
classic cheese fondue 30, 31
coconut split pea curry 42, 43
curried quinoa broccoli bowl 40, 41
easy bread 206, 207
fasolada 26
hearty chickpea stew 27
Indian-style vegetable curry 38, 39
lentil and sweet potato dal 44, 45
one-pot brioche 210, 211
pear and almond cake 212, 213
popcorn 204, 205
ratatouille 24, 25
rice pudding 218, 219
Sicilian caponata 22, 23
stewed pineapple with vanilla 214, 215
tortellini stew 32, 33
vegetable soba noodles 20, 21
vegetable tagine 28, 29
yogurt cake 208, 209
vermicelli pasta
Moroccan lamb and chickpea chorba 186, 187
vin jaune
coq au vin 80, 81

W

walnuts
    braised veal with carrots and walnuts 172, *173*

waterzooi 58, *59*

West African-style beef stew 141

whipping cream
    Flemish veal stew 180, *181*
    pork tenderloin in cream sauce 124, *125*
    turkey and butternut squash stew 98, *99*

white beans
    quick and easy cassoulet 118, *119*
    veal and chorizo bean stew 166, *167*

wine
    Basque-style veal stew 178, *179*
    beef Bourguignon 138, *139*
    beef hot pot 156, *157*
    Belgian-style fish stew 58, *59*
    bouillabaisse 54, *55*
    braised veal with carrots and walnuts 172, *173*
    Catalan-style seafood stew 68, *69*
    chicken fricassee 90, *91*
    classic cheese fondue 30, *31*
    coconut-lime mussels 60, *61*
    coq au vin 80, *81*
    creamy veal and vegetable stew 170, *171*
    easy monkfish casserole 52, *53*
    mushroom risotto 18, *19*
    osso buco 162, *163*
    pork tenderloin in cream sauce 124, *125*
    pork tenderloin with orange-honey glaze 130, *131*
    Provençal beef stew 158, *159*
    rabbit in mustard sauce 104, *105*
    sausages and sauerkraut 112, *113*
    slow-braised leg of lamb 196, *197*
    turkey and butternut squash stew 98, *99*
    veal Marengo 176, *177*

Y

yeast
    easy bread 206, *207*
    one-pot brioche 210, *211*

yogurt
    beef biryani 160, *161*
    lamb tikka masala 188, *189*
    pear and almond cake 212, *213*
    yogurt cake 208, *209*

Z

zarzuela 68, *69*

zucchini (courgette)
    beef biryani 160, *161*
    Colombo-spiced pork and sweet potato stew 132, *133*
    Moroccan lamb and chickpea chorba 186, *187*
    Moroccan-style fish stew 56, *57*
    one-pot salmon 48, *49*
    pistou soup 14, *15*
    Provençal beef stew 158, *159*
    ratatouille 24, *25*
    stuffed zucchini and tomatoes 120, *121*
    Thai shrimp curry 64, *65*
    tortellini stew 32, *33*
    vegetable tagine 28, *29*

PHOTOGRAPHY CREDITS

Martin Balme (food stylist Lucie Dauchy): 97, 173; Fabrice Besse (food stylist Bérengère Abraham): 17, 29, 41, 43, 49, 51, 55, 57, 59, 69, 77, 87, 99, 101, 103, 113, 117, 121, 123, 125, 127, 131, 133, 137, 143, 149, 153, 157, 159, 161, 165, 167, 171, 175, 177, 179, 181, 183, 187, 189, 191, 197, 201, 205, 211, 213, 215, 217, 219; Emanuela Cino (food stylist Anne Loiseau): 37, 91, 129; Guillaume Czerw (food stylist Alexia Janny-Chivoret): 163; Charly Deslandes (food stylist Juliette Lalbatry): 31, 105, 107, 139, 195; Sophie Dumont (food stylist Delphine Lebrun): 73, 79, 95, 151; Amandine Honegger (food stylist Sylvie Rost): 19, 25, 53, 63, 141, 199; Marie-José Jarry (food stylist Bérengère Abraham): 61; Nicolas Lobbestael (food stylist Mélanie Martin): 207; Olivier Ploton (food stylist Catherine Moreau): 81; Aline Princet (food stylist Isabelle Guerre): 23, 39, 75, 89, 145, 193; Laetitia Vasseur: 83; Fabrice Veigas (food stylist Isabelle Guerre): 21, 35, 65, 67, 85, 111, 115, 147, 169; Fabrice Veigas (food stylist Pauline Dubois-Platet): 45, 119, 155, 209.

RECIPE CREDITS

Bérengère Abraham: 28, 60, 122; Anna Austruy: 106; Amandine Bernardi: 16, 27, 50, 56, 68, 76, 78, 86, 102, 112, 120, 124, 126, 136, 142, 148, 158, 164, 166, 168, 170, 178, 180, 182, 188, 200, 204, 210, 212, 214, 216, 218, 130, 132, 141, 160, 152, 156, 174, 176, 186, 190, 26, 180, 48, 58, 98, 100, 116, 40, 42; Pauline Dubois-Platet: 44, 118, 154, 208; Isabelle Guerre: 20, 22, 34, 38, 39, 54, 62, 64, 66, 72, 74, 84, 88, 92, 93, 114, 144, 146, 192; Béatrice Vigot-Lagandré: 24, 198; fonds Larousse: 16, 30, 80, 82, 90, 94, 96, 104, 138, 140, 162, 172, 194, 196; Delphine Lebrun: 150; Anne Loiseau: 36, 52, 128; Mélanie Martin: 206; Clémence Roquefort: 18.

RECIPE NOTES

Unless otherwise specified:
- Butter is unsalted.
- All spices are freshly ground.
- Eggs and individual vegetables and fruits, such as carrots and apples, are assumed to be medium-sized.
- All sugar is white caster (superfine) sugar and all brown sugar is cane or demerara (turbinado).
- All cream is 36–40% fat heavy whipping cream.
- All milk is full-fat (whole) at 3% fat, homogenized and lightly pasteurized.
- All yeast is fresh.
- All salt is fine sea salt.

Cooking times are for guidance only, as individual ovens vary. If using a conventional oven, follow the manufacturer's instructions concerning oven temperatures.

All herbs, shoots, flowers, and leaves should be picked fresh from a clean source.

Because some species of mushrooms have been known to cause allergic reaction and illness, do take extra care when cooking and eating mushrooms and do seek immediate medical help if you experience a reaction after preparing or eating them.

Exercise a high level of caution when following recipes involving any potentially hazardous activity, including the use of high temperatures and open flames and when deep-frying. In particular, when deep-frying, add food carefully to avoid splashing, wear long sleeves, and never leave the pan unattended.

Some recipes include raw or very lightly cooked eggs, meat, or fish, and fermented products. These should be avoided by the elderly, infants, pregnant people, convalescents, and anyone with an impaired immune system.

When no quantity is specified, for example of oils, sugars used for finishing dishes, or for deep-frying, quantities are discretionary and flexible.

Both metric and imperial measures are used in this book. Follow one set of measurements throughout, not a mixture, as they are not interchangeable.

Always check labels of condiments and other pre-prepared ingredients and choose a brand that suits your dietary requirements.

MEASUREMENT NOTES

All spoon and cup measurements are level, unless otherwise stated.
1 teaspoon = 5 ml; 1 tablespoon = 15 ml.

Australian standard tablespoons are 20 ml, so Australian readers are advised to use 3 teaspoons in place of 1 tablespoon when measuring small quantities.

Phaidon Press Limited
2 Cooperage Yard
London E15 2QR

Phaidon Press Inc.
111 Broadway
New York, NY 10006

Phaidon SARL
55, rue Traversière
75012 Paris

phaidon.com

One Pot: 100 Simple Recipes to Cook Together originates from *Cocotte* by Amandine Bernardi
© Larousse 2024

© 2025 Phaidon Press Limited

ISBN: 978 1 8372 9060 4

A CIP catalogue record for this book is available from the British Library and the Library of Congress.

All rights reserved. No part of this publication may be reproduced, stored in a retrieval system or transmitted, in any form or by any means, electronic, mechanical, photocopying, recording or otherwise, without the written permission of Phaidon Press Limited.

Commissioning Editor: Emilia Terragni
Project Editor: Michelle Meade
Production Controller: Gif Jittiwutikarn
Cover Design: Julia Hasting
Interior Design: Hans Stofregen
Layouts: Cantina

Printed in China

ACKNOWLEDGMENTS

Phaidon would like to thank James Brown, Marnie Lamb, João Mota, Ellie Smith, and Ana Teodoro.